Winning the Innovation Race

Winning the Innovation Race

LESSONS FROM THE AUTOMOTIVE INDUSTRY'S BEST COMPANIES

Lee A. Sage, Ernst & Young LLP

JOHN WILEY & SONS, INC.

New York ➤ Chichester ➤ Weinheim ➤ Brisbane ➤ Singapore ➤ Toronto

This book is printed on acid-free paper. ♾

Published by John Wiley & Sons, Inc.

Published simultaneously in Canada.

Library of Congress Cataloging-in-Publication Data:

Sage, Lee A.
Winning the innovation race : lessons from the automotive industry's best companies /
Lee A. Sage, Ernst & Young LLP.
p. cm.
Includes index.
ISBN 0-471-33346-8 (cloth : alk. paper)
1. Automobile industry and trade—Technological innovations. I. Ernst & Young. II. Title.

TL240.S246 2000
658.4'06—dc21

99-048040

Printed in the United States of America.
10 9 8 7 6 5 4 3 2 1

Contents

Preface		vii
Acknowledgments		xiii
Chapter 1	Introduction	1
Chapter 2	Encouraging Innovation	27
Chapter 3	Maximizing Employee Potential	47
Chapter 4	New Product Development	60
Chapter 5	The Power of Process Innovation	85
Chapter 6	Technology	101
Chapter 7	Innovation in the Supply Chain	122
Chapter 8	Managing and Applying Knowledge	141
Chapter 9	Leading the Race toward Innovation	160
Chapter 10	Winning the Innovation Race	174

Appendix A The Concept Automotive Industry Project 177

Appendix B The Automotive News PACE™ Award Recipients, 1998–1999 209

Notes 227

Index 233

Preface

Today, there is wide recognition that innovation has the power to reshape the way we live and work. In the United States, the popular media report the successes of entrepreneurs associated with technological breakthroughs, and regulators bristle whenever corporate practices threaten the business community's ability to create and implement new technology. Innovations in computing, telecommunications, medical procedures, and pharmacology have brought all of us very far, very fast.

Innovation is a welcome antidote to the waves of downsizing and mergers that have swept through many industries. Downsizing produced short-term improvements for the bottom line, but rarely improved the long-term outlook. And most mergers and acquisitions have failed to generate net improvements; many, in fact, have failed to cover their costs. Innovation, in contrast, creates real value for customers. As a result, executives are turning to innovation and new product development as the generator of profitable growth.

But while the impact of innovation is generally understood, the mechanisms for fostering and managing it in the workplace continue to puzzle executives. The problem is that there is much more to innovation than any one person can understand or interpret. Innovation has many faces. No one sees them all or has enough insight to probe the connections between them. This book aims to correct part of this defect. It describes the forms that innovation takes in industrial organizations, and how truly excellent companies manage to sustain innovation through effective management. The following chapters explain:

- The role of innovation in value creation and competitive advantage—how innovation gives companies the power to attack quality, cost, and time-to-market simultaneously, thereby providing superior value to customers.
- The key elements of innovation in new product development.
- How companies build and sustain an innovative culture over time.
- The tangible rewards of innovation.
- The essential role of executive leadership.

Innovation, like profit, is part of a much larger picture, and a consequence of many complex actions and judgments. For companies that know how to sustain it, innovation is an outcome of how they approach employees, business processes, and technology development. Thus, innovation is a function of people, processes, and technology. Outstanding companies innovate in all three dimensions. Each dimension of innovation is explained through text, data, and examples of outstanding companies—the best of the best—in the U.S. automotive supply industry.

ORIGINS

My own interest in innovation has grown out of years of consulting with managers and executives in the automotive industry, and from being a co-founder of the Automotive News PACE™ Awards. PACE—Premier Automotive Suppliers' Contributions to Excellence—jointly presented by Ernst & Young LLP and *Automotive News,* recognizes innovation in the automotive supply industry, a dynamic sector of the economy that currently provides some one-seventh of all employment in the United States. The program grew out of our discovery that these suppliers were constantly reinventing themselves, taking risks, assuming new responsibilities, fostering innovation, and partnering in new and creative ways. Further, the industry is operating in the teeth of rapid change.

Since its beginning in 1994, the PACE Awards program has enabled us to examine the thinking and the management practices of the best of these supplier organizations, and to make them known to others. Companies involved with the PACE program, especially the finalists and winners, have demonstrated practical know-how about the meaning of innovation, its implications, and the practices that lead to it. Most important, we've learned how innovation translates into value, company differentiation, and business success.

The automotive industry might seem to be an odd place to look for examples of world-beating approaches to innovation. After all, the automobile has been around for more than a century. Its configuration and underlying technologies are closely related to those of vehicles manufactured in the early twentieth century: the power source remains overwhelmingly the gasoline-burning internal combustion engine; power is directed to the wheels through a transmission; the passenger space is enclosed on a four-wheel platform, with a steering wheel, throttle, and other controls made available to the driver. The engine generally is enclosed in a front section while a rear enclosure is available for baggage.

By the standards of most other industries, the automobile should now be an ordinary commodity, with few differentiating features, sold almost entirely on the basis of price—perhaps by direct mail. Like the television set, the refrigerator, and the water heater, the automobile should now be viewed as nothing more than a utilitarian device. Consumers should have outgrown the "romance of the road" and any personal identification with this contraption generations ago.

Yet, far from becoming a commodity product, the automobile has retained its hold over the hearts and pocketbooks of customers worldwide. Despite most outward appearances, virtually every system of the modern automobile (and truck) is the product of ongoing innovation: ABS brakes, air bags, fuel injection, electronic ignition, radial tires, computerized controls, catalytic converters, electromechanically controlled side mirrors, impact-absorbing bumpers, space-saving spare tires, halogen headlamps, and auto-dimming mirrors represent significant innovations, and most are now standard equipment. Others, like collision-avoidance radar, GPS locators, night vision capabilities, and hybrid power systems are no longer on the dim horizon but are entering many manufacturers' list of options.

For every innovation under the sheet metal of today's vehicle, however, we can find several more in the design and manufacturing processes for that vehicle—and its thousands of components, systems, and subsystems. Collectively, these process innovations have slashed the time it takes to design and assemble parts and products, and have resulted in higher quality, better performance, and lower costs for both OEMs and end-use customers.

■ ABOUT THE PACE AWARDS

PACE examines how today's leading suppliers give birth to innovative products and services. Its goal is to identify, analyze, and honor those innovators—and to learn from them in the process.

Any company that contributes products, materials, or services directly to the manufacture of cars or trucks can apply for the PACE Award. A distinguished panel of industry, financial, business, and academic leaders review and evaluate the corporate practices and innovations of all applicants against demanding criteria, and conduct site visits to finalist companies. All applicants receive a valuable report of findings and benchmarking data; finalists receive a customized and confidential report that allows them to directly compare their practices against those of other world-class suppliers across key operating measures.

More information on PACE is available from www.ey.com/PACE.

The changes in automotive supply industry are emblematic of the turmoil and competitive pressures sweeping many other industries—globalization, consolidation, and overcapacity; pressure for greater speed, quality, technological innovation, capital productivity, environmental standards/safety; and the need to form closer relationships with customers. We hope readers will find that lessons learned in this one industry will be applicable to their own businesses.

Lee A. Sage

Acknowledgments

Ernst & Young colleagues who were instrumental in bringing together the concepts in this book include Rob Evans, Jenny Febbo, Tom Griesser, Frank Khoshnoud, Pam LeMasters, Andrea Mackiewicz, Ajay Patel, Ralph Poole, Mike Shoffstall, and Christian Wright.

The PACE judges, who serve as field investigators in the awards program, have provided a treasure trove of data and examples of excellence in practice. Among these, special thanks go to William Sharfman, Tom Hachiya, Scott Whitlock, and William Krag, who read the manuscript and suggested improvements. So too have several company managers we interviewed in developing this book, including Brian Wilkie, Kim Shepperd, Dave Rozsnowski, Gary Corrigan, Chuck Jones, Dan Cavanaugh, Fred Bauer, Connie Hamblin, Sally West, Greg Still, Karl Schein, Peter Jones, Aly Badawy, Beth Bernthal, and Glenn Gardner. Thanks also to our PACE Awards cofounders at *Automotive News*, especially Keith Crain and Peter Brown, for their vision and commitment to innovation.

In the book-building effort, Richard Luecke of Salem, Massachusetts, interviewed most of the managers cited and helped develop the manuscript for publication.

Finally, my sincere thanks to the hundreds of managers, engineers, scientists, and technicians with whom I've had the good fortune to work with over the years. They have been responsible for many of the product and process breakthroughs that make our lives better today. They continue to teach us how innovation happens and how it can be sustained.

L.A.S.

Introduction

The innovators, the attackers, will always have the advantage.

Richard Foster
Innovation

In 1992, Delphi Automotive's Steering Systems Division in Saginaw, Michigan, manufactured one of the best hydraulic-assisted steering systems available. A complex assembly of seals, pumps, valves, and hoses, this technology for power steering had been around for several decades, and it did the job very well. Years of incremental improvement had brought it to a state of high perfection—both in design and manufacturing—and many employees recognized opportunities for continued improvement.

Instead of staying on this familiar and successful course, however (and despite internal opposition), the division's leadership urged it onto a risky and unexplored new trajectory. General Manager Don Runkle and his successor, Paul Tosch, recognized how one automotive system after another was moving from mechanical to electronic, and how each transformation led to fewer parts, greater reliability, and better performance. In their view, the same was destined to happen to steering.

Any move in this new direction would be disruptive and difficult. New competencies in motors, electronics, control algorithms, and sensors would have to be acquired or developed from scratch, with no assurance of success. Many of the division's engineers questioned the need for change and the diversion of investments that could have been directed to improvements to the current product. But sitting still was equally risky. According to one company executive, "If we hadn't developed this technology—and someone else had—we could have lost our entire business."

In the end, management decided to make the perilous leap. Several years later, a team of newly hired engineers and personnel from the traditional business introduced E-Steer™, a full-performance electronically assisted steering system with major benefits for automakers and final customers. E-Steer replaced all hydraulics with a power-assisting electric motor uniquely designed for the purpose. Heavy and space-consuming pumps, hoses, fluids, and seals were eliminated, reducing weight as well as parts and assembly costs. Since the system was powered by the automobile's battery, and not by an energy-draining engine belt, E-Steer improved mileage. And to the delight of manufacturers and drivers alike, the steering characteristics of any E-Steer-equipped vehicle could be easily tuned through its programmable microchip—even after installation.

Good things have happened for Delphi Saginaw Steering Systems and its employees since the introduction of its innovation. E-Steering has been adopted for vehicles produced by Opel, Volkswagen, and Fiat, and selected for the new GM Delta platform on which new Sunfire and Cavalier cars will be built. The division has remade itself from traditional design and manufacturing to high tech, and employees are excited about being part of the change. "You can see the excitement," says one executive, "when an engineer comes running and tells you, 'I've gotten it to work! Come drive the vehicle and tell me what you think.'"

Innovations like the one just described permit companies to attack quality, cost, performance, and time to market simultaneously—delivering superior value to customers and changing the nature of competition. Consider the case of personal computers (PCs). Every time you replace your CPU, monitor, and printer you cannot help but notice two things: the cost—even considering inflation—is less and equipment performance is substantially greater. That old system you bought in 1995 for $2,800 probably ran at 100MHz; the 1999 equivalent runs at three times the speed. This new machine also came out of the box with built-in features that had to be added externally and at extra cost to the old model (if they existed at all): a 56K modem, a zip™ drive, and a much faster CD-ROM or DVD drive. Best of all, the new, more capable, and more reliable machine cost about 30 percent less than the old clunker in inflation-adjusted dollars.

Many of these cost and performance improvements are not the result of innovations in the fullest sense. They are refinements to existing components and processes (e.g., packing more power onto microprocessors through continued miniaturization, reducing the number of parts that have to be assembled into an automobile). But others are innovations in the best sense of the word. The Zip drive allows us for the first time to store huge quantities of data on a single diskette. The Internet provides a new method for communicating and acquiring information. The catalytic converter cuts auto emissions to a fraction of earlier volume. The onboard computer assures that each cylinder in your car's engine gets the proper mixture of air and fuel.

The list of true innovations that have found their way into your PC and automobile alone over the past five years could fill several pages of this book. But we are less interested in recounting technical breakthroughs than in describing the process of innovation and identifying practices that leading companies use to innovate on a continuing basis.

Five major trends appear to drive the need for continual innovation:

1. *Globalization.* As original equipment manufacturers (OEMs) and their suppliers go global, their ability to innovate can provide a critical advantage in launching new products, gaining market share, and securing important relationships worldwide. Globalization impacts us in many ways. Supply chains now span the globe. Processes must be designed to encompass the needs of global brands and operations. Technology must provide round-the-clock access to markets and sources of knowledge.

2. *E-commerce.* The Internet is breaking down boundaries, helping to free companies from old business practices and relationships. Though most applications of e-commerce are in the fledgling stage, it will surely become a viable sales channel in the years ahead and alter the relationships between customers and producers.

   A major consequence of the Internet is the ability to exchange information without heavy investments in infrastructure. Another is the growing shift of market power from producers to consumers. As consumers gather more information and knowledge, they are better able to bargain. Currently, 25 percent to 35 percent of the car buyers access the Internet for information and pricing before going to a dealer showroom. At the same time, dealer employee turnover is approaching 70 percent per year. The result is a smarter buyer dealing with a less experienced and informed salesperson.

3. *The power of new products.* Beating competitors to market with new products that anticipate customers' desires is the key to winning business today. Leading companies look for ways to innovate the new product development process itself, since doing so leverages

their ability to plan and introduce winning new products.

4. *Supply chain cost reduction.* Innovations in the management and development of supply chains and supply chain relationships can make some companies highly valued as partners. Supply webs are beginning to replace supply chains, supplanting the package offerings preferred by manufacturers with the offerings valued by customers.
5. *Connectivity.* Boundaries between economies, industries, organizations, and functions are becoming blurred. Networks are forming where walls once stood. Communications between supply chain participants are becoming more rapid and free-flowing. This connectivity catalyzes innovation.

■ WHAT WE MEAN BY INNOVATION

Most people use the word innovation loosely, applying it to anything seen as new. In our PACE Awards program, we've had to be more rigorous in our definition. We describe an innovation as any product, process, or technology that has not been seen before, is adopted by customers, changes the basis of competition, and transforms the innovator's business for the better. The following subsections consider each requirement in detail.

➤ Has Not Been Seen Before

Whenever my colleagues and I look at a product, a service, or processes, we ask this question: "Is this really different from anything we've seen before?" If it is, how different is it?

Many of the innovations the PACE judges see during their company visits are remarkably new—a fact that inspired one judge to say, "One of the reasons we keep doing this year after year is that it makes us just plain happy to see a lot of creativity and cleverness being applied successfully." These innovations make lots of customers happy as well.

An innovation is, as its Latin root implies, something new (nova) or newly applied in a product, process, or service. The well-known story of Thomas Edison's first successful incandescent light bulb provides a good example. Electric arc lighting had been around years before Edison's breakthrough in 1879, but sustained illumination from an electric current running through an element had previously not been achieved. Several months after Edison's initial laboratory success, the first commercial application of this new lighting technology took place aboard the steamer *S.S. Columbia*. The application itself was an innovation that displaced the oil lamps previously used. In the closed spaces below deck, smokeless and flameless electric lamps represented a major improvement in performance and safety.

In some cases, creative adaptation from one industry to another represents a legitimate innovation. The products of

CREATIVITY OR INNOVATION?

The difference between creativity and innovation can be confusing. 3M, a company that knows about both, explains it this way: "Creativity is thinking up new things. Innovation is doing new things. The relationship between the two is clear: Innovation is the practical application of creativity. Both are necessary for 3M to succeed and grow."

Source: The 3M Innovation Center.

the automotive industry are complex electromechanical systems on wheels; like a magnet, the modern automobile has attracted and incorporated innovations that originated elsewhere: computer controls, fiber optics, electrochromics, and cellular telecommunications, to name just a few examples.

➤ Adopted by Customers

Newness is not enough to qualify as an innovation in our view. An innovation must also be accepted by customers, otherwise it is nothing more than a clever idea. Customer acceptance tells us that the innovation has real value. It is beneficial either as a source of efficiency, as a productivity enhancer, as a relationship-builder, or as a product differentiator. A true innovation isn't only stunningly new, it also provides an answer to a real commercial question. In some cases, it answers a question that customers have not yet thought to ask; in this sense, the innovation fulfills a latent need. For example, the remote entry function now available in many automobiles links the automobile with the garage door opener and with the home lighting and security system. Before its introduction, customers did not recognize the convenience or need for this device. Now that it is an option on many vehicles, we wonder how we got along without it.

➤ Changes the Basis of Competition

True innovations rewrite the rules of the game. They affect how things are done, designed, manufactured, priced, or marketed. In many cases, they change standards and raise customer expectations. Things are no longer the same once the innovation enters the marketplace. The introduction of an innovation puts competitors on the defensive, forcing them either to react or to do business from a position of weakness.

We are used to thinking of new technologies as the only innovations that change the basis of competition, but a new process can be just as powerful. The annual revenues of Dell Computer Corporation have skyrocketed to over $12 billion in only 13 years—a remarkable achievement. Dell sells more than $14 million worth of PCs each business day over the Internet alone!

The innovation that made Dell a huge success was not a powerful new chip or a more user-friendly operating system—it was founder Michael Dell's process of directly distributing custom-built PCs made from off-the-shelf components. While IBM, Compaq, and others were laboring to design and manufacture many of their own components—and pushing these products through traditional retail and corporate sales channels—Dell was carving out a direct channel to customers and refining a process to quickly assemble and deliver made-to-order machines. With no dealer markups, no component manufacturing operations, and no inventory pipelines to worry about, the new company entered the field with a significant cost advantage.

Having no inventory pipeline allows Dell to operate with negative working capital and to quickly and inexpensively convert from model A to model B without having to work off weeks of now-obsolete inventory. Its direct relationship with customers was the icing on the cake. This new process essentially redefined the PC business and is now being applied in their business direct channel. Organizations outside the PC industry are now studying and applying Dell's principles with more zeal than we have seen since the discovery of the Toyota Production System in the early 1980s.

One PACE winning company, Johnson Controls, Inc. (JCI), views its reputation as an innovator as an important differentiator between itself and its competitors, giving it a leg up in securing new contracts. Because of JCI's ability to create auto interior concepts that delight end users, its OEM customers are more than pleased to include JCI as a working partner. As Marketing Vice President Mike Suman tells us, "When we can go to an OEM with data from its customer—the consumer—about an idea we've been developing, and then apply that idea, we create a win-win scenario."

➤ Transforms the Innovator's Business for the Better

True innovations can do great things for a company and its shareholders. They may lower production costs, increase product performance above those of competitors, create product differentiation, or help the company increase its share of industry relationships. Some breakthroughs make it possible for the innovating company to exit a moribund business and move into one with greater growth potential. Corning Incorporated, one of the oldest companies in the United States has repeatedly benefited from this characteristic of self-reinvention.

For more than a century, innovations developed in Corning's R&D laboratories have allowed the company to expand out of once lucrative businesses that had become marginally profitable, and into others. Corning was the original supplier of light bulbs to Edison (now General Electric). When light bulbs became commodity products, the company exited that business in favor of others of its own creation, including the cellular ceramic substance used in all automotive catalytic converters worldwide.

Today, Corning holds more than 200 patents for emission-control products and processes used in gasoline, diesel, and alternative-fuel vehicles. In March 1999, it introduced a new substrate that will make it possible for automobile manufacturers to reduce emissions by as much as 70 percent over then-current national standards, including pending federal Super Ultra Low Emission Vehicle (Super ULEV) standards scheduled to take effect in the year 2004. According to the company, hot, untreated exhaust gases will pass through the substrate, where they will react with the catalyst and convert to harmless gases and water vapor.

Corning was also the world leader in the production of TV tubes, a business that once, in the words of a company executive, rained "money from the sky." As that business matured, it attracted low-cost Asian competitors. Corning's margins and market share plummeted. A major technical breakthrough, however, made it possible for the company to abandon that commoditized business in favor of one with far greater potential. Innovations in the field of fused silica optical wave guides by three Corning scientists—Donald Keck, Robert Maurer, and Dr. Peter Schultz—gave the company commanding leadership in the new and more lucrative field of fiber optics.

Not every innovation changes the innovating company for the better. Some involve transformations in people, processes, and technology that are more costly and disruptive than beneficial. Innovation is thus potentially a liability as well as a competitive necessity, and the process consumes resources. It's the job of corporate leaders to determine which ponies they should ride and which they should avoid, a subject discussed in the book's final chapter.

■ DISCONTINUOUS AND INCREMENTAL INNOVATIONS

Scholars generally classify innovations into two categories: discontinuous and incremental. Discontinuous or breakthrough innovations are infrequent and result in dramatic cost or performance improvements. Jet propulsion was a discontinuous innovation in the field of aviation that opened the door to major performance improvements, enabling threefold increases in airspeed. The transistor developed by Bell Laboratory scientists was, likewise, a discontinuous innovation, opening the door to a huge leap forward in the world of electronics. Transistors enabled the miniaturization (or scaling) that now packs a contemporary laptop with computing power hundreds of times greater than was available in vintage mainframes that occupied dozens of cubic feet and consumed great quantities of electricity during the 1960s.

Incremental innovations, in contrast, are "innovations at the margins"—either small steps forward or new applications. Thus, the first computer-on-a-chip semiprocessor represented a discontinuous innovation; the next generation chip that simply piled more switches on the same chip represents an incremental innovation. Typically, incremental innovation occurs frequently and under the auspices of operating units instead of corporate R&D. Though they lack the *pizazz* of real breakthroughs, incremental innovations often have the same cumulative effect on cost and performance, as demonstrated by the experience of the petroleum refining, microchip design, and other industries.

Figure 1.1 indicates how discontinuous innovation takes the form of a sudden and major leap forward in either

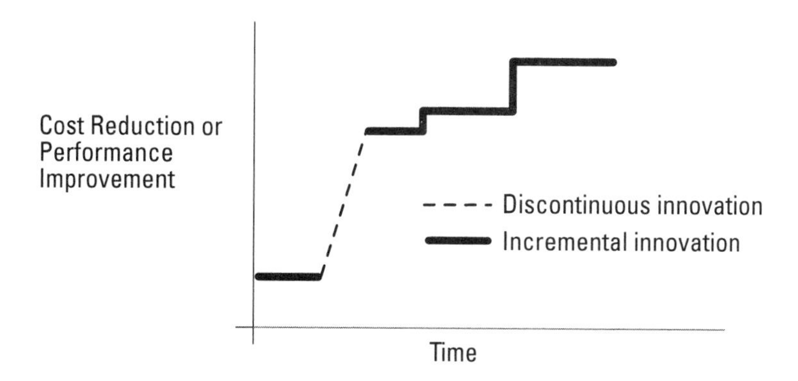

Figure 1.1 Discontinuous and incremental innovation over time.

INNOVATION AND CONTINUOUS IMPROVEMENT

The line between incremental innovation and continuous improvement is sometimes blurred. Kaizen, suggestion systems, quality circles, and other improvement themes add to a company's operational effectiveness and are a necessary companion of innovation. But they are not innovation. They do not affect strategy; innovation does. Today, every company needs a successful program of continuous improvement to stay in the game, but it requires sustained innovation if it hopes to be a leader.

performance or cost reduction. Incremental innovation, however, accomplishes smaller improvements through progressive steps over time. More often than not, a technology is subject to both types of innovation.

■ THE INNOVATION PROCESS

Although the general public thinks of innovation as a product or a single event, people who work with it regularly understand it as a process. To view it as a product or event would require us to believe that innovations appear suddenly from the blue. All experience, however, points to a long course of work and discovery involving 10 to 20 years for discontinuous innovations and several years for the incremental types.

The recognition of innovation as a process is good news for managers. The past dozen years or so have provided them with many practical tools for improving work processes; making them faster, better, and cheaper; and improving the quality of their outputs. Many of these managerial tools can be applied to the process of innovation.

As we encounter innovations in industrial companies, we can identify six key steps or stages along the bumpy road that begins with someone's bright idea and a commercial product or new process that has real value. These conform closely to the stage-gate milestones popularized by Robert Cooper.[1] They are:

1. Idea generation.
2. Recognition and qualitative evaluation.
3. Business evaluation.
4. Prototyping.
5. Testing and validation.
6. Production ramp up and marketing.

The first two steps of this process constitute what many in R&D refer to as the "fuzzy front end" of innovation, shown in Figure 1.2. Since these are the least well defined, they merit special attention here.

➤ Idea Generation

Often, innovation begins with an individual—a person with an idea. This person may be a customer, a salesperson, an engineer, or bench scientist working in the company's R&D lab, a production employee who is frustrated with the way the process is organized, or—in one case we studied—a summer intern.

The power of a single idea to create a new business or to alter the basis of competition is remarkable. In one observed case at Prince Corporation (now part of Johnson Controls, Inc.), a single idea led to a major new product line—the HomeLink® Universal Transceiver—a system that

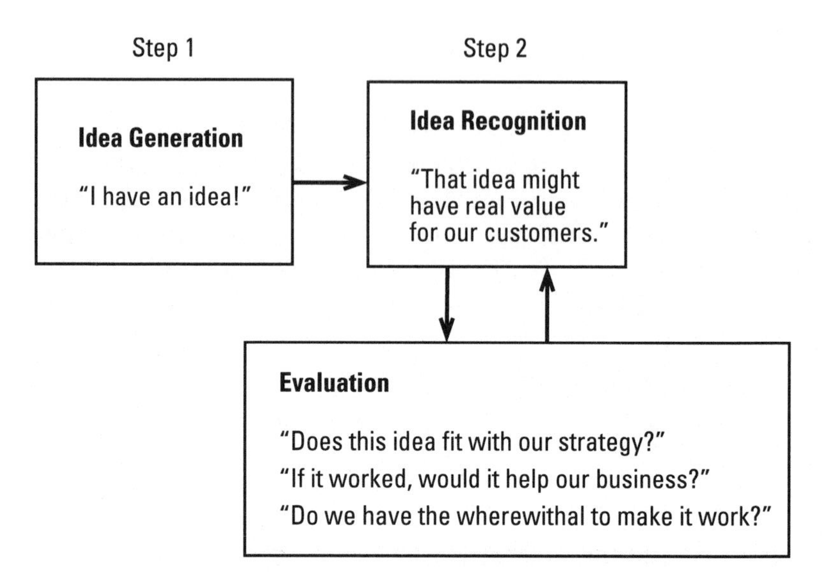

Figure 1.2 The fuzzy front end of the innovation process.

allows drivers of more than 5 million currently operating automobiles to remotely open garage doors, operate their door locks, and activate lights and security systems in their home from a single control pad integrated within the automobile. But even the initial idea depended on other ideas for the solution of all the technical and market issues.

New ideas often emerge from the intersection of a known technology and a customer need. The intersection is the trigger. At other times, innovation comes from recognizing a customer need better than the customer does. One of our PACE judges, Scott Whitlock, likes to use this example:

> *A customer wants us to make product X with material Y. We analyze and find that material Y is incompatible with the heat-resistance requirements for the product. Insight: the customer wants us to use material Y because it is made from post-consumer recycled materials. The inspiration is that*

material Z is also a post-consumer recycled material, but one that also meets our heat-resistance requirements.[2]

Innovative ideas can also be kindled when a number of creative minds are put around a problem. One of our favorite examples is the development of CorteX®, an advanced, energy-absorbing material developed by JCI for use in vehicle overhead systems, door panels, and other interior features. How CorteX® was conceived and developed provides a useful lesson on how management can stimulate new and profitable ideas.

CorteX® was a direct response to a larger JCI corporate strategy: to produce zero landfill waste. Waste products are both expensive and fast becoming socially unacceptable. As a result, many enlightened companies and industries are aiming for "closed loop" systems that build new materials from recycled products, then reuse these same materials when their useful lives are over.

In Germany, where the "green" movement is particularly strong, DaimlerChrysler is moving toward the point where every part and fluid in one of its Mercedes-Benz vehicles is not only recyclable, but is recycled when those vehicles are eventually scrapped. The same development is happening in the United States, where major OEMs such as Ford Motor Company are requiring or giving preference (all else being equal) to suppliers whose products have significant recyclable content.

With CorteX®, JCI has taken the concept two steps further: (1) the material is made from recycled material (used carpeting and plastic soft drink bottles), and (2) the material will eventually be recycled for the same purpose—the ultimate closed-loop system.

For the development of JCI's new material, the company identified 30 engineers it viewed as competent and creative in the materials area, set them up in an unused company building in Holland, Michigan, and asked them to come up with a new and suitable car interior material that would help move the company toward its zero waste goal.

The group spent months analyzing material applications for various vehicles. Company executives gave their full support and encouragement to the team, calling them regularly for updates. "We couldn't have done this without their backing and motivation," said team leader, Peter Elafros. "There were times when the phone would ring constantly. They wouldn't be calling to ask how we were and what was new. They wanted to know how the project was going."[3] JCI adopted the same approach with a program called SIT (Seat Innovation Team). In this case, the company selected a handful of people representing different functions (market research, manufacturing, design, etc.), and put them in a "skunkworks" for one year with the mission of producing as many new ideas for improving automobile seats as possible. In the course of the year, the SIT team produced more ideas than anyone would have imagined, and these are currently being integrated into the company's line of auto seating. Here, the process of innovation was more important than any single output.

The team approach to innovation is deeply embedded at JCI. As Mike Suman, Vice President of Marketing, likes to say, "Invention by itself is only about 20 percent of the total value [of a potential new business]. If you don't have a designer to design it, and an engineer to prototype and build it, and somebody to promote and sell it, it's not going to go anywhere."

➤ Recognition and Qualitative Evaluation

Once a good idea surfaces, someone has to recognize its merits—either as a product that customers will value, or as a new process capable of reducing cost or improving quality in some fundamental way. The "recognizor" also needs to have the clout or the organizational connections to enlist the broader base of support and funding to move that idea down the long, often bumpy road to commercialization.

The second step in our process model, therefore, is idea recognition. Typically, the recognizor is an older colleague, a supervisor, or the head of a project team—a person with both technical know-how and a broad understanding of the company's strategy and markets. He or she may be in another area, but spots the idea and has an insight about its potential significance. This person recognizes both the technical merits of the innovation and its commercial potential.

Implicit in the recognition step is some level of qualitative evaluation as to the fit of the idea with company strategy and the fit of the idea with the company's technical capabilities or markets. For an idea to survive this second process step, immediacy is essential. Toss a good idea into a bureaucracy of gatekeepers and it's bound to fizzle.

This is exactly what happened to Hewlett-Packard in the late 1980s when it centralized many of its new product decision-making processes—a major departure from the decentralized approach that went hand in glove with the company's progress over the years. Innovators suddenly found their projects stymied by a thicket of committees and approval boards. The situation became so bad that founder Bill Hewlett briefly returned from retirement to straighten out the mess, which in his prescription was to return to the company's tradition of decentralization.

A similar situation was reported in May 1999 regarding Microsoft. How could a company with over 40 percent margins and $400 billion in market capitalization have to reinvent itself? Nevertheless, Bill Gates and Steve Ballmer recognized that the company had too many layers and too much sludge in the product development process. The results were late-to-market products and stifled personnel.

Our PACE judges have not observed a single instance in which a successful innovation passed through multiple layers of approval committees. This observation explains why small companies are so good at sustained innovation. In these companies, very little separates decision makers from employees with good ideas. Large companies only have this immediacy when they are decentralized or have a culture of informal communications that moves ideas more directly and rapidly than the organizational chart would suggest.

JCI, like many other companies, uses a stage-gate process that filters all ideas through review boards set up within each of its operating units. These review boards have the job of quickly killing ideas that are either flawed or inappropriate for the company. Quick killing combined with idea recognition assures that scarce R&D resources are not wasted on bad projects or spread too thinly over too many projects. Approval at the review board stage clears the way to formal funding and development. We'll return to this important subject in Chapter 4.

■ INNOVATION'S REWARDS

Managers often ask, "Don't I already have enough to do without managing something else?" Yes, these executives already have plenty to do: round after round of budgeting and planning; countless turf disputes that must be settled, and resettled; and ongoing efforts to improve employee productivity. Manage these issues and the business will keep on running, and may even grow by 5 percent each year. But manage your business so that it crackles with innovation, and your world will change dramatically and for the better.

In the late 1970s and early 1980s, Ford Motor Company was not a happy place to be. The company was hemorrhaging cash, losing $1.5 billion in 1980 alone. Customers and noncustomers alike viewed its new models as unremarkable in design and of poor quality. In 1978, Ford recalled more vehicles than it produced. Morale was at rock bottom.

Then, following the prescriptions of W. Edwards Deming, the company began to change. Quality became "Job 1." Designers were told to start with a clean sheet of paper and create a new midsize car that would excite them and other drivers. Line workers and independent auto mechanics were formally invited to give their advice on how the new model could be made easier to assemble and service. Teams of Ford managers and employees benchmarked over 50 vehicles in the same product class to determine "best in class" on some 400 features deemed important to customers.

Almost 500 employees from different parts of the company were brought together into a new, organically structured car development team unlike any other in the company's long history. Most things about this new car project were different, untried, and viewed by many as extremely risky. Marketing staffers feared that the new car's streamlined design was too radical a departure from the boxy models to which Ford's customers had become accustomed. They pleaded for caution and compromise: Make the car different, but not too different.

The outcome of this project was the 1986 Ford Taurus, a car that sold extraordinarily well, won kudos from the automotive press, and pulled the venerable Ford Motor Company out of its death spiral. Before long, Ford was the most profitable of the Big Three. And the streamlined design over which company marketers had lost so much sleep became the design that all competitors eventually mimicked.

The Ford experience is not an isolated case. Our PACE finalists over the past several years point to corporate rewards in key categories:

➤ *Sales growth.* PACE finalists have registered significant and consistent sales growth. Further, revenues generated by new products (those less than two years old) are far ahead of those experienced by peer group companies and by industry in general. Average annual sales growth of PACE finalists for 1993–1997 was 9 percent, compared with only 5.9 percent for the top 25 public suppliers.

➤ *Sales from new products.* For 1999 PACE winners, 20 percent of sales revenue came from products three years old or less. Three winners reported that sales from new products represented 70 percent of total annual revenues.

➤ *Quality.* The quality performance of PACE finalists is high and continues to improve across several metrics. For example, between 1993 and 1997, these innovative companies cut their percentage of scrap by 59 percent. Likewise, the percentage of rework and the number of customer defects notices both declined by impressive degrees (see Figure 1.3).

➤ *Speed.* Thanks to process innovations, PACE finalists have cut the time from concept to marketplace. Even

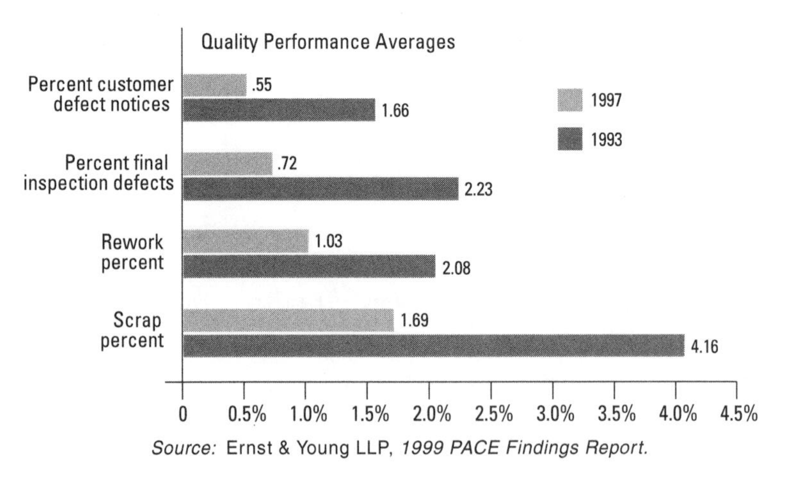

Source: Ernst & Young LLP, *1999 PACE Findings Report.*

Figure 1.3 Quality performance measures.

more impressive is that virtually all (99.2 percent) product deliveries reach customers on time. This performance is critical in an industry that increasingly demands just-in-time performance. Time consciousness is also reflected in fast changeovers and in downtime efficiency, which has measurably improved over just a few years (see Figure 1.4).

➤ *Product development leadership.* These technically proficient companies are assuming a greater share of

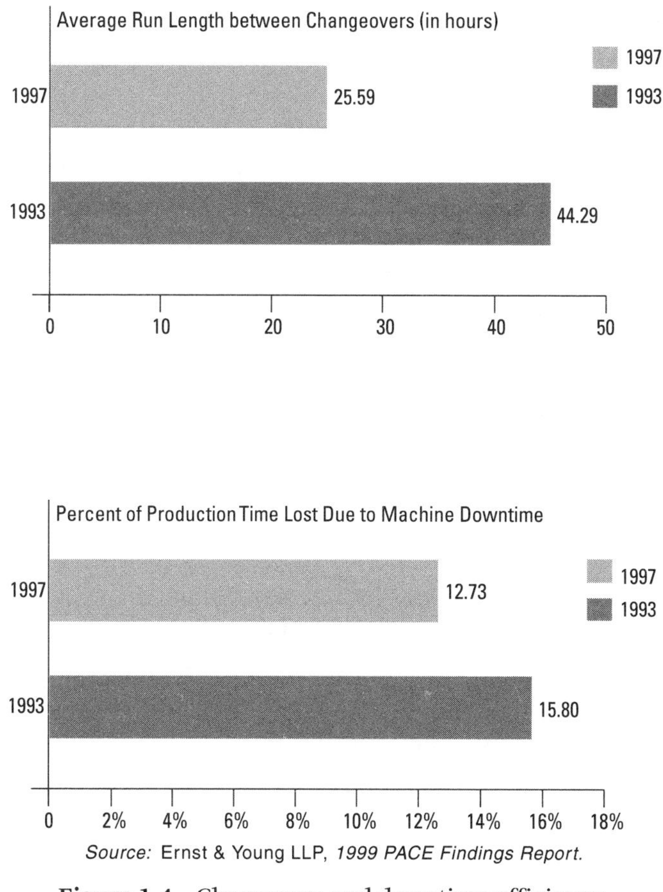

Source: Ernst & Young LLP, *1999 PACE Findings Report.*

Figure 1.4 Changeover and downtime efficiency.

product development with respect to the OEMs they serve. PACE data indicates that "black box" designs represented slightly more than half of their products (i.e., product designs for which they, as suppliers, were fully responsible). During that same year, only 8 percent of their new products were fully specified by customers. The remaining percentage of new products were designed and developed with customers.

➤ *Profitability.* For shareholders, and for employees whose compensation is in some way pegged to the bottom line, profitability is the key indicator of corporate performance. Here again, our PACE finalists did exceptionally well, scoring an average annual earning before income tax (EBIT) of 14.4 percent.

➤ *A greater share of industry relationships.* Innovation results in more successful competition for a share of industry relationships and opportunities to serve more ways and deliver more value.

Innovation pays. And time dedicated to managing the innovation process will produce higher returns than any other activity. Perhaps equally important are the psychic profits of innovation. People like to work at a place that's recognized as a leader and as an organization that's doing great things!

■ THE INNOVATION BUILDING BLOCK

Our studies have concluded that results like those just described are no accident, but are the consequence of many complex actions and judgments that, taken together, create innovation on a sustainable basis. Consequently, we represent innovation through a three-dimensional model comprising people, processes, and technology. Truly outstanding companies innovate along all three dimensions as shown in Figure 1.5. Put these dimensions together, and you have a solid basis for sustained innovation.

➤ People

No organization can innovate consistently without a workforce capable of stepping up to the demanding pace of current competition, which in many industries is brutal and becoming more so.

Our findings show that real innovators rely heavily on employee training, empowerment, and rewards and recognition systems to create wellsprings of innovation. In almost every situation we have studied, we find an individual who wouldn't take no for an answer, who added one more piece of knowledge, and who was willing to take a risk. The seeds of innovation grow best where individual employees are stimulated and actively encouraged to bring forward good ideas. In Chapter 2, we'll take a close look at Gentex Corporation of Zeeland, Michigan. Under the leadership of Fred Bauer, the company has created an environment that produces a reliable stream of innovative products.

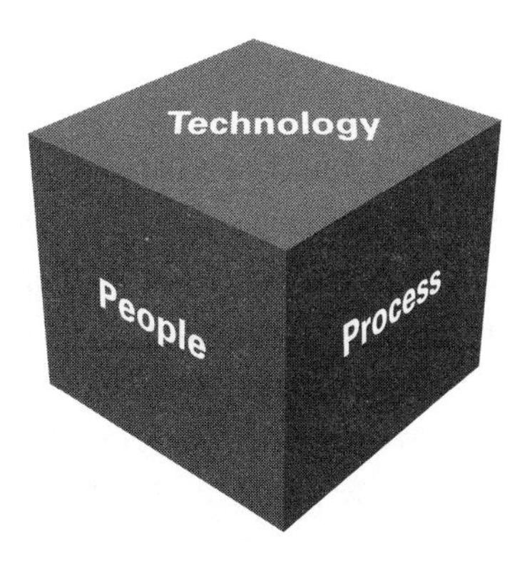

Figure 1.5 The innovation building block.

➤ Processes

Innovative companies seek a rigorous process for everything they do.

A process is a series of interrelated activities that convert inputs to outputs. In the absence of good processes, managers and employees burn up their time just getting the work done. A flawed process is like a leaky, beat-up old steam engine that chugs and chugs but wastes as much energy as it produces. Its handlers are forever patching leaks, lubricating friction points, and applying temporary fixes. There is no time for thinking creatively or for innovating.

A good process liberates people from the mundane elements of work, establishes clear decision criteria, and gives them time to innovate. Earlier, we discussed the new product development process used throughout Johnson Controls, Inc. (JCI), a repeat PACE winner that creates new products at a blistering pace. Virtually every PACE winner adheres to a well-tested process. Rigor and decisiveness are necessary for the incremental innovations that companies work at on a continuing basis.

➤ Technology

Innovative companies are adept at creating and importing new technology. Technology is the traditional venue of industry-altering innovation. Beginning with Edison's establishment of an "invention factory" at Menlo Park, New Jersey, in 1876, the great industrial companies and universities of the world have pursued innovations in well-equipped laboratories staffed with scientists and technicians. Many rely on periodic technical breakthroughs for corporate self-renewal. This has been the case for Eastman Kodak, DuPont, Corning, 3M, and dozens of others around the globe.

The origin of Eastman Kodak, late in the nineteenth century is associated with its founder's technical innovations.

George Eastman came into the photographic business in the 1880s as an amateur with an enterprising sense of the business. Within a short time, he developed process technologies for mass-producing glass photographic plates at a much lower cost than his competitors could achieve. His interest then turned to the creation of photosensitive film, a blockbuster product innovation that created a huge new market in both Europe and North America. Prior to this technical breakthrough, photography had required expensive equipment and specialized skills; Eastman made it a simple and affordable pastime for the masses.

Eastman and his scientific and engineering teams went on to develop and patent dozens of new process technologies for supporting the huge and growing demand for photographic film. The history of Eastman Kodak in the decades that followed is punctuated by technical innovations great and small, each renewing the firm's vitality. The ability to continue innovating will be an absolute necessity in the new age of digital imaging.

■ IS YOUR COMPANY AN INNOVATOR?

A quick and easy approach to assess your own company's innovative capabilities is to answer the following questions:

- ➤ Do competitors react to what you do and what you offer customers? Are they forced to change based on your actions?
- ➤ Have you increased market penetration and profit margins in the face of intensified competition?
- ➤ Are you able to accomplish more with fewer resources and less time and space?
- ➤ Have you demonstrated leadership in strategically targeted areas?

- ➤ Have you been able to anticipate customer needs in strategically targeted areas?

If you answered "yes" to each of these questions, you probably don't need this book. Otherwise, read on.

■ WHAT'S AHEAD

In this book, we examine technological innovation as it relates to people, technology, and processes. Organization, culture, and leadership receive equal attention. We will take you inside outstanding companies to identify the practices, structures, and attitudes that encourage employees to make a habit of seeking new and better ways for doing things. Finally, we look at what successful leaders do to win the innovation race with their competitors.

Encouraging Innovation

> Innovation is exciting. Innovation is fun. And innovation is dangerous at times, [but] if it doesn't kill you, it makes you stronger.
>
> Fred Bauer

Does your company encourage innovation? Ask corporate executives that question and you'll hear a unanimous response. "Of course we encourage innovation. We believe in risk-taking, and we look to our employees for better ways of doing things."

It's true that the concept of the empowered employee has largely replaced the industrial age notion of the rank-and-file drone—at least in the business press, in corporate pronouncements, and in the speeches of CEOs. Saying that you encourage innovation is one thing, but creating the rewards, attitudes, and organizational structures that open the doors to innovation is another. And few corporations do it as well as Gentex Corporation of Zeeland, Michigan.

With 1,400 employees and over $222 million in annual sales (1998), Gentex is the dominant supplier of electrochromic mirrors to the worldwide automotive market, controlling 90 percent of that growing business. Its ability to innovate and to replace one technology with another is one reason its annual growth rate over the past 10 years has averaged 30 percent. Investment wizard Peter Lynch once called the small company a "10-bagger"—one whose stock price would grow 10-fold in a relatively short time. Gentex is also a three-time winner of our PACE award, recognized in 1995, 1996, and 1998 for its unrelenting work in its core technology.

If you have ever had your night driving vision impaired by the headlights of a following vehicle—either from directly behind or in the passing lane—you can appreciate the utility of electrochromics, a technology developed by Gentex. Electrochromics uses sophisticated circuitry and sensors to automatically vary the reflectivity of auto and truck mirrors. Its Night Vision Safety® (NVS) mirrors provide an active, crash-avoidance safety feature, the same designation given to antilock brake systems. These high-tech mirrors detect glare from following vehicle headlamps and dim their effects before the driver ever notices. Reflectivity is reduced in proportion to the amount of glare, and accomplished in a way that optimizes driver vision.

The enhanced driver safety achieved with NVS mirrors has induced many of the world's automakers to begin equipping their vehicles with Gentex products. Currently, vehicle models produced by General Motors, Chrysler, Ford, Southeast Toyota Distributors, Gulf States Toyota Distributors, Mercedes-Benz, BMW, Toyota/Lexus, Nissan/Infiniti, Opel, Fiat, Bentley, Rolls Royce, Honda, Hyundai, Daewoo, and Kia offer Gentex NVS mirrors as either a standard or optional feature.

The interior NVS mirror introduced in 1987 was not Gentex's first innovation, nor its most recent. The company has since developed several advanced-feature NVS mirrors that incorporate, variously, an electronic compass, map lights, remote keyless entry control, and electronics for turning a vehicle's head- and taillights on and off at dusk and dawn.

The company made another major step forward in 1997 when it introduced "aspheric" exterior NVS side mirrors. These are curved mirrors that greatly increase the driver's field of view while being small enough to meet styling and aerodynamic requirements. These mirrors provide nearly three times the field of traditional flat exterior mirrors and twice that of convex mirrors, virtually eliminating the age-old problem of the driver's "blind spot."

Combined with electrochromic dimming technology, these aspheric mirrors represent an important breakthrough in crash protection; and several large automakers plan to phase these mirrors into their product lines as standard equipment over the next several years.

Gentex scientists and engineers are currently working on other applications for electrochromic technology, including windows for architectural applications, atrium glass, automotive window and sunroof glass, and sunglasses. Even as those applications are being sought, the company is working to improve both its patented electrochromic technology and its own manufacturing processes with the goal of improving performance and optical quality, and reducing cost.[1]

Chrysler honored Gentex in 1998 with its Platinum Pentastar Award for supplier quality and overall corporate achievement, making it the only component supplier to receive the honor five years running.

The question for us in this chapter is: What is it about the working environment at Gentex that produces innovations like electrochromics and keeps them coming? We looked to the company's mission statement for the answer:

To be a smarter organization; a world class manufacturer with superior products and service driven by a supportive work culture that encourages people to innovate, excel and continually improve every aspect of the business.

Nice sentiments, but we need to look beyond the words to the structures and the programs that produce results. When we do, we find that Gentex has created an innovation-friendly environment primarily through five approaches, all of which appear to be common to innovative companies:

1. A visible, top-level commitment to innovation.
2. Reward and recognition programs that align individual effort with corporate innovative goals.
3. A deliberate effort to attract and retain innovative people.
4. The elimination of fear in the workplace.
5. Organizational "discomfort" with the status quo.

■ TOP-LEVEL COMMITMENT TO INNOVATION

From Fred Bauer's "look-back" bonus to the minority report of Motorola, you will see repeated illustrations of visible, top-level commitment to innovation throughout this book. That commitment takes many forms:

➤ *Recognition.* It is important for company leaders to recognize innovation and innovative behavior. Success is widely acknowledged. We need more acknowledgment of the ideas and behaviors that were not successful. Playing with new ideas, probing for new applications, and working with customers in new ways are behaviors that should be encouraged through recognition.

➤ *Visibility of leadership.* Leaders who spend time in the development area demonstrate the importance of the innovation process and the people who do the work.

➤ *Barrier blasting.* Corporate leaders should help knock down walls between people and help innovators cut through the bureaucracy. Everyone has heard stories of a good project hamstrung because they were three percent over budget or because managers couldn't make decisions. It's the job of top executives to clear away these barriers, turn people loose, give them challenging targets, and ensure that they are working toward customer desires, not departmental desires. Harvard professor John Kotter has taught us the role of leadership is to establish direction, align resources, and inspire and motivate employees. Who does this in your organization?

■ REWARDS AND RECOGNITION

People who study organizational behavior remind us that "we get what we measure." We also get what we pay for. Rewards and recognition programs, when thoughtfully engineered, align the interests of employees with the corporate strategy. So, when the company wants more innovations, rewards and recognition programs can help get them. Johnson Controls recognizes innovative accomplishments at its quarterly meetings. Other companies have quarterly gatherings for people with ideas. Gentex's approach is heavily based on financial incentive: it shares the risks and the rewards with employees in transparent ways. Following this philosophy, salaries for its engineers and scientists are average or slightly below average. However, these employees can earn bonuses as great as their current salaries if corporate financial performance is high, which is the case in most years. As CEO Fred Bauer told us:

> *I've done this entrepreneurship thing for a lot of years, and, remembering what turned me on to it, we've tried to set up a*

system where our professional associates can become wealthy. I call it "enlightened greed." We share the risk and the wealth with them. The mechanisms are multi-level. Starting salaries are average, or maybe even below average when they join us. Our base salary is nothing huge. Then what we have is a profit sharing system—more so than most companies. We take a pretty large slice of our pretax profits—a percentage that's fairly constant at around 20 percent, so that people don't think that we're playing games. We create a pot out of those profits and pay everyone a flat bonus, regardless of their position. We make these payments every quarter. So, a substantial portion of a person's pay depends on how well we do as a company.

PAY INCENTIVE FOR PACE WINNERS

Among PACE award winners, both salaried and hourly employees see a significant portion of total compensation in the form of incentives. The actual percentages have been fairly stable over time (Figure 2.1).

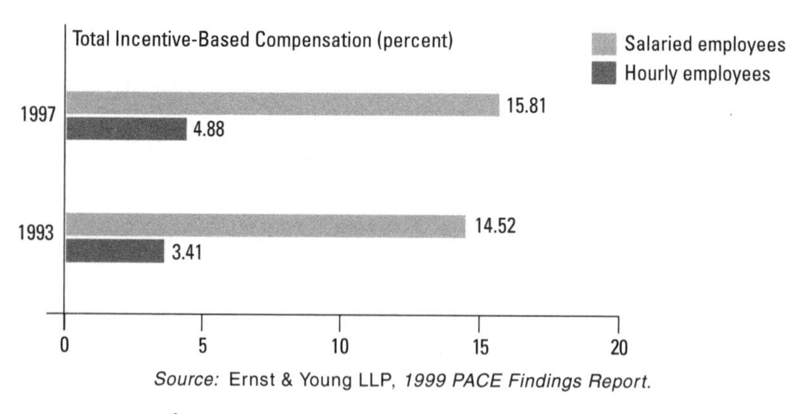

Source: Ernst & Young LLP, *1999 PACE Findings Report.*

Figure 2.1 Pay incentive for PACE winners.

Gentex supplements its incentive system with a generous stock option program for all salaried employees, which begins the day the employee is hired—a very unusual practice. Options awards are much larger than those of most companies and additional options are awarded on the basis of each individual's contributions, as determined through the annual performance review. Of course, stock options in a company whose stock is not going up aren't worth much as an incentive. But Gentex sales and profits have grown at a 30 to 40 percent annual rate for more than a decade, making employee stock options extremely valuable, and making many employees, including mid-salary employees, wealthy. The average Gentex associate has, in fact, earned more than 100 percent of salary through the stock option program. And associates who have been with the company for seven years have seen the value of their company's shares increase 60-fold!

Individual achievements are further encouraged through "look-back" bonuses. "If someone makes a great discovery or earns a patent, or does something surprising and unusual," says Bauer, "we'll simply write him a check. These range from $500 to as high as $15,000, and we have done as many as ten of these look-back bonus in one week."

For Bauer and for Gentex, look-back bonuses are a way of saying "thank you" to people who have done something extraordinary that will contribute to the company's future growth. They are also a mechanism for getting managers to look for things that have "gone right" and not, as in most companies, for things that have gone wrong. "And for every look-back bonus we give out," Bauer estimates, "we give out at least four times as many personal compliments: 'You're doing a great job,' or 'We really appreciate the work you're doing.' These probably do more to energize people than the money."

The net effect of these programs, according to CEO Bauer, is that when a person asks:

> *"If I really put out, if I really sweat and take these problems home with me at night, am I going to be rewarded?" the answer will be "Yes, this company will reward extra effort." In fact, a huge percentage of our associates are wealthy. At most big companies, they reach the opposite conclusion. After about ten years, people realize that they can kill themselves working for the company and they probably won't be rewarded, at least not big-time or in a personal way that means anything. And so they express their energies and inventiveness elsewhere—through hobbies and community activities in which they develop great passions.*

Money is not the only stimulant for innovation. Public praise and recognition are also effective. 3M Corporation, one of the all-time innovation champs, has developed many ways to recognize innovative behavior and achievement among its cadre of technical and scientific personnel. Researchers who succeed in making major contributions are inducted into the Carlton Society (named after the company's first degreed laboratory worker and fifth president, Richard P. Carlton). The Golden Step Award is conferred on teams that create and market products that produce $4 million or more of profitable sales in one year. Like IBM and many other firms, the corporation confers fellowship status on high-achievement scientists, a status that lends both recognition within the scientific community and greater freedom to follow new lines of inquiry.

➤ Dual Career Ladders

3M provides a choice of career tracks as a reward for its successful innovators. They can advance through technical or general management or, alternatively, stay in the laboratory and follow another track that leads to Corporate Scientist. Motorola supports a similar program—in effect a "technical ladder" through which scientific, engineering, and technical personnel can advance in status and compensation without being managers. Not everyone, after all, wants to

THE OUTWARD-LOOKING COMPANY

Success creates many self-destructive behaviors. One is the tendency to become inward-looking. If yours is the greatest steel maker or electronics maker—or whatever—hubris encourages employees to believe that the solution to any problem exists somewhere inside the company itself. Being pleased with yourself and your work becomes a comfortable but self-deluding habit. "We have the best designers, the best scientific staff, the best marketing people . . ." If looking inward for solutions becomes a habit, the company will be impervious to new ideas.

Gentex is the best in its field, but finds ways to be outward-looking. It maintains two company planes and encourages people who want to talk to a customer or supplier, or to attend a professional conference, to get on the plane and go. "Get out and bump around," Bauer tells them, "that's the only way to find out what's going on."

At Monroe Auto Equipment Company, every business traveler finds a reminder on the front of his or her airline ticket packet to keep alert to new products, technologies, and processes that could help Monroe compete more effectively.

Benchmarking is an important institutional approach to getting people to look outward. At a recent Innovation Forum we sponsored, representatives from Motorola remarked that benchmarking helped them to understand Motorola's performance relative to others; break down resistance to change; and understand how fast and how steep the improvement curve must be.

be a manager or would be effective as a manager. Motorola's managerial and technical ladders are essentially parallel.

➤ We Want Your Ideas

Companies also create a climate of innovation when they tell employees that their ideas are important and when they actively seek them. Employee suggestion systems are in place at 77 percent of PACE finalists. More important, these companies act on more than half of the suggestions received—a remarkable increase over the past several years.

Dana Corporation, the world's third-largest automotive components maker, has worked hard to develop and institutionalize a system of employee suggestions. It asks each of its employees to offer two suggestions each month. With 86,000 employees worldwide, that's a lot of suggestions. And, remarkably, it is very close to meeting its goal and has acted on 80 percent of those suggestions.

■ ATTRACTING INNOVATIVE PEOPLE

"Innovation begins," according to Fred Bauer, "with the quality of people you hire, and we're very selective—much more so than the normal company." Gentex tries to hire technical and professional people who:

➤ *Like variety.* Because its products incorporate several technologies, employees must be interested in learning about many things. Once the company brings technical personnel onboard, it attempts to mold them into "hybrid people"—technical people who understand enough about the company, its business, and its markets to recognize the business opportunity in a new idea and can wear many hats.

By design, Gentex R&D keeps in close proximity to manufacturing. This gives technical people a good idea of what the real world is like and shapes their inventions to be more useful. According to Fred Bauer,

> *We have lots of very smart people in this country, but if they work in a vacuum and aren't regularly exposed to information about what would be valuable to customers, the result will not be very positive. That may explain why the results produced by many independent R&D groups are so pitiful. The groups that produce the most are usually in close contact with the business and its market. That's why we physically locate our R&D close to manufacturing, and it's why we encourage our technical people to interact with customers and to attend our sales meetings. This helps them feel the pulse of what's going on.*

This characteristic is not unique to Gentex. Several companies we've talked with express the same interest in employees who can function across different enabling technologies, who can span organizational silos, and who understand customers and how to communicate with them.

➤ *Are willing to share the risks.* People who insist on certainty in their compensation don't fit in well at Gentex, where total compensation is heavily skewed toward individual and corporate performance.

After you've met a few innovators, you begin to realize that they are different from most people. Peter Drucker maintains:

> *Successful innovators use both the right and left sides of their brains. They look at figures. They look at people. They work*

> *out analytically what the innovation has to be to satisfy an opportunity. They go out and look at potential users to study their expectations, their values, and their needs.*[2]

In general, innovators are intuitive people who can see things that the average person doesn't see and doesn't even look for. They have an internal hunger for knowledge and a "best solution." Dave Longaberger, who passed away recently, was one of these very different people. Born with a dyslexia, he didn't graduate from high school until he was 21 years old. Nevertheless, he founded and managed a highly successful company called Longaberger Basket. Located in the small town of Dresden, Ohio, the company developed a market strategy similar to that of Tupperware—women-to-women sales through home parties. But Dave's operation was also unique. He created a "demand pull" manufacturing operation long before people in North America began reading about it in business books. He also set up a tremendous merchandising approach, having busloads of people tour his plant, eat lunch in his restaurants, and buy products in his company stores. From these simple concepts, he took his company from nothing to about $750 million in annual sales. Dave was also a great leader. People followed him because he was trustworthy, consistent, and had their best interests in mind; they also admired his intuitive and positive spirit.

Ken Stork, who recently retired from Motorola, is another great innovator. Intelligent, highly intuitive, *and* analytically skilled, Ken had a remarkable ability to identify and connect the critical factor associated with a new concept. We often joked that once Ken saw the first 20 pieces of a jigsaw puzzle he could describe the rest of the picture.

Innovators cannot produce in a negative or constrictive environment. Like young children, workers who are told "no" too often eventually learn not to challenge, not to push against the edge, and not to seek new answers. Bureacracy, lack of decisiveness, and constant rejection repel them. Just like flowers in fertile soil, ideas grow better and faster where the environment for innovation is encouraged.

■ ELIMINATING FEAR

W. Edwards Deming put his finger on one of the most important deterrents to innovation when he told managers that they had to drive fear out of the workplace. Doing so is, in fact, one of the late Dr. Deming's 14 principles of quality.

Fear of failure and fear of pushing a viewpoint unpopular with management have a chilling effect on the creation and development of innovative ideas. Fear creates a bunker mentality, encouraging people to keep their heads down lest they lose them.

Failure is the constant companion of innovation. Almost by definition, only a small percentage of new ideas for products, processes, and technology ever pan out. Most fail in the initial stages of idea formulation. Others are unable to prove their worth as they seek customer applications. In still other cases, early prototypes simply fail to work. Intuition is sufficient to warn us that employees who suffer recriminations for well-intended failures will not produce new ideas. Like the proverbial cat who put his paw on the hot stove, they will not be burned twice. Gentex's approach is to avoid dwelling on failure. "If you do that," according to Bauer, "they won't be inclined to stick their necks out again." An "innovation friendly" environment separates ideas from people. In this environment, ideas can fail while people survive.

New ideas are often unpopular, and unpopularity can repress their development. This is particularly problematic when an innovation has the potential to cannibalize existing product lines and the jobs and bonuses they support—

when they challenge the status quo. As Machiavelli warned centuries ago, ". . . the reformer has enemies in all those who profit from the old order." Delphi Saginaw Steering faced this problem when it set about developing internal competencies in electronics, electric motors, sensors, and computer controls. This revolution took place within a company populated almost entirely by mechanical engineers, many of whom had spent their careers with hydraulic systems that would be displaced by the new technology. Unstinting top-management support and good personnel practices turned a potential revolt into wholehearted compliance for Delphi Saginaw Steering.

At Dana Corporation, the managers and engineers who participate in the company's process of technology innovation understand that they are free to suggest new initiatives, even when they fly in the face of long-standing company practice. Several years ago, when the process was first being developed, that freedom was untested. More than a few employees were nervous about one issue thought to be organizationally untouchable: the development or acquisition of a piston company. The lack of a piston unit had been a sore point for years among Dana engineers. But no one had had the intestinal fortitude to confront senior management about the problem. So when one engineer stood up at a meeting and told the CEO that Dana needed a piston company to be competitive, many wondered how soon this fellow would be cleaning out his desk. "We thought that this guy would be looking for a job the next day," recalls Chuck Jones, Dana's technology manager. Instead, the company's president and CEO explained, almost apologetically, the problems they had had finding a suitable acquisition candidate. That response removed any cloud of fear that may have existed among the people charged with finding and developing innovative technologies for the company.

Motorola has done much to eliminate innovation-killing fear from its workplaces by maintaining a tradition of open dissent that allows workers, scientists, and engineers to disagree with their superiors. Brian Wilkie of the company's advanced vehicle systems division, refers to this tradition as one of "structured open-mindedness." Employees can file a minority report when ideas they consider valuable to Motorola's future fail to receive support from their immediate superiors. These reports, in the words of former Chairman Robert Galvin, are intended "to assure that the initial or current non-supported project received a further hearing or were not forgotten for later support."[3] Similiarly, 3M maintains a "court of appeal" on innovative projects. Likewise, the chairman of Continental AG periodically identifies himself as the executive sponsor of one or more innovative product ideas. This gets the chairman involved in the organization at a deeper level, communicates the importance of innovation for all employees, and helps eliminate resistance.

EVERY FAILURE BRINGS US CLOSER TO SUCCESS

Thomas Edison exemplified the right attitude about failure during his systematic but frustrating search for a suitable filament material for his first incandescent light bulb. Over the course of months, Edison and his "insomnia squad" of laboratory assistants experimented with hundreds of metal or fiber materials. One after another, they would attach the thread-like strands of material to two poles of an electrical circuit. The entire works was then covered by a glass bulb, the air removed to create a vacuum, and the power was switched on. As each failed in turn, Edison pushed on to the next material, satisfied in the knowledge that he had eliminated one more dead end. Eventually, he found one that worked—carbonized cotton thread.

Fred Bauer shared this story about fear and failure at his own company. About 10 years ago, when Gentex was still struggling to develop electrochromic technology, one board member complained "We can't afford to continue losing money on that project—we need to cut it off." At that time, the project was draining the company of cash and making its financial situation perilous. But the potential of the technology—*if* it could be made to work—was substantial. So instead of cutting funding, Bauer shared the board members' concern with the electrochromics project leader, giving him this advice: "Watch your expenses and try lots of different things." The project leader went back to work and, following his boss's advice, quickly tried 20 different things. One worked, and that breakthrough now accounts for the majority of Gentex's revenues and earnings.

Dürr Industries provides an environment in which innovative employees feel free to follow the scent of a potentially important breakthrough without fear of failure. Century-old Dürr Industries is the global leader in designing and building continuous flow industrial ovens for baking paint onto various vehicle bodies and occasionally parts and panels.

Dürr's oven had undergone a series of incremental refinements; it was a highly reliable and effective product, but had not changed fundamentally for years. The result, in the words of Greg Still, engineering director at Dürr's Plymouth, Michigan facility, was that "To customers, it had become indistinguishable from the competition." Something had to be done to develop an oven capable of delivering a step-change in performance to customers. But how?

In 1994, free-thinking Dürr personnel representing engineering, manufacturing, sales, and field operations participated in brainstorming sessions aimed at breaking the current paradigm of oven design. As a matter of company practice, all constraints were taken off the problem, and no Dürr approaches were placed off-limits. "We identified a number of principles that could be part of a new, step-change product," Still told us. One of these was the amount of air circulating in the "hold zone" of the oven. High air turnover was an accepted approach to maintaining a constant baking temperature in the hold zone. The task force decided to overturn that principle and consider ways to reduce air circulation. Doing so would help reduce two long-standing problems in oven operations—energy costs, and the air-borne dust that entered the hold zone. Going a step further, the task force wanted the new oven to cure coatings applied to dissimilar components or materials—steel, several types of plastics, and aluminum. Early indications were that such an oven could not be built. So what better group to enlist for the project than a bunch of novice engineers who were not invested in the current technology—people who didn't know any better?

Dürr has a history of recruiting newly minted engineers from universities in and around Michigan. Normally, these new hires are assigned to the engineering department, where they learn from experienced employees how things are done at Dürr. For this project, however, several new engineers were assigned directly to R&D, where they would work with seasoned Dürr managers. There, the young engineers were given a much longer leash. As General Manager David Meynell explains:

> *They asked a lot of questions. They interviewed our customers, they interviewed paint manufacturers, they attacked the dirt in paint problem . . . they asked "why" a thousand times. They plowed on [and] they wouldn't take no for an answer.*

In the end, the young engineers and their senior R&D mentors proposed some untried and unaccustomed solutions. The result of their efforts was the Radiant Floor Construction paint oven, which won a 1998 PACE award. "What they came up with is not the prettiest product in the industry," according to Meynell, "but, by golly, it works very well." This three-zone curing oven heats dissimilar materials simultaneously and primarily uses radiant instead of convection heat. Air continues to circulate, but in a closed-loop duct structure that surrounds the hold zone and never comes in contact with the painted product. The result has been highly favorable: reduced dirt deposits on coated surfaces; a 10 percent reduction in gas and 22 percent lower use of electricity; and greatly reduced oven maintenance.

It is this type of environment—one in which even new employees feel empowered to ask tough questions and propose radical solutions—that supports sustained innovation. And it pays off. Dürr has received orders from GM, Ford, and DaimlerChrysler for its new oven, and continues to make improvements.

■ ORGANIZATIONAL DISCOMFORT

"The certain knowledge that you're to be hanged in a fortnight tends to concentrate the mind wonderfully," Dr. Samuel Johnson once said. Companies and their employees likewise appear to concentrate best when the danger level is high. As the head of engineering at Delphi Steering told us in the opening story of this book, one of the two forces that drove his company to push forward into the new and uncertain field of electronically assisted steering was the nagging fear that the entire business might be lost if a major competitor were the first to capture it.

In the fast-paced world of technology-driven industry, paranoia is a useful form of survival insurance. As Intel® cofounder Andy Grove says, "In this business, only the paranoid survive." Many of the innovative companies we see share this anxiety and worry about being caught napping by a key competitor or being blindsided by a new "disruptive" technology originating outside their own industry. Fred Bauer confesses to losing sleep at night over this and attempts to makes all Gentex employees feel what he calls "organizational discomfort" with the status quo. "Guys like me get uncomfortable if everybody is feeling comfortable."

Organizational discomfort is a good antidote to the hubris and complacency to which successful companies are naturally prone. Discomfort imparts a sense of urgency and an attitude favoring positive change and innovation. In this slightly electric environment, employees at all levels maintain personal radar sensitive to opportunity recognition. They are alert to the needs of customers, customers' customers, and opportunities for change. Making fellow employees feel that discomfort is an important part of executive leadership, a topic to which we return at the very end of this book. Our PACE finalists and winners all display a productively restless energy. They are comfortable with change, with ambiguity, with creative destruction. They're uncomfortable with comfort, always a bit fearful of losing their edge and losing momentum. They overcome that fear through positive activity: proposing, trying, and even failing.

■ WHERE DOES YOUR ORGANIZATION STAND?

This chapter has described five characteristics of an innovation-friendly environment and how some companies have put them in place. How does your company stack up against this list?

1. Is there a visible, top-level commitment to innovation?
2. Do you have reward and recognition programs in place to encourage innovation?
3. Have managers and your human resources department been proactive in attracting and retaining innovative people?
4. Do the people who try but fail get their fingers slapped or a pat on the back and encouragement to "keep trying"?
5. Are people too comfortable with their current success?

How you answer these questions will indicate a great deal about the innovative environment of your company.

Maximizing Employee Potential

Mankind, I am sure, is born to learn.

Charles Handy
The Age of Unreason

If the climate of a company is open to change, then an innovative idea has an opportunity to germinate and develop. It will only succeed, however, if the idea receives sponsorship at a level capable of providing resources and support. This interplay of idea generators and structures of support is common to the companies that sustain innovation. But nothing happens until some*one*—and we emphasize *one*—gets an idea.

Much ink has been spilled over the past few years on the importance of teams in just about everything, from product development to process reengineering to strategy development. Nevertheless, almost every winning innovation we've seen begins with *a single person*. In many cases, these individuals become champions of a new way, a new idea, a new plan. If they have leadership ability and enjoy the respect of their peers, they gather people around them who can help develop their ideas and advocate on their behalf.

Once this happens, teamwork and multidisciplinary activities can come into play.

If the initial spark of innovation depends on individuals, it follows that organizations must try to upgrade their knowledge and skills, provide them with opportunities to innovate, and create support structures that allow them to develop potentially promising ideas. They must also open channels for employee participation and clear away organizational barriers that stifle creativity and protect the status quo. In this chapter, we will explore these approaches to maximizing the innovative potential of individual employees through the following organizationally sponsored activities:

- Employee training.
- A spirit of employee participation.
- Creation of free flows of information.

Benteler Automotive Corporation, a 1999 PACE winner, developed an innovative rear axle thanks to a combination of these approaches. Contributors to the new product came from the entire organization—from managers, engineers, and toolmakers on the shop floor. Other companies are using the same approach.

■ EMPLOYEE TRAINING

Education and training pay. Economist Gary Becker of the University of Chicago has estimated that the rate of return on educational investments for individuals ranges between 12.5 percent and 25 percent. Anything in that range would be an excellent return. But what about the return for companies that invest in education and/or training? The National Center on the Educational Quality of the Workforce at the University of Pennsylvania conducted the first detailed study of this important question. This organization surveyed approximately 3,000 business establishments with more than 20 employees.

Across all industries, the study found that increasing the average employee's reading or math comprehension by just one year is associated with a 8.6 percent productivity increase. Service industries experience slightly higher productivity increases (11%); in fact, training investments by service companies are three times more effective in improving productivity than are equal investments in plant and equipment.[1]

MOTOROLA'S INVENTION LEADERSHIP PROGRAM

Motorola was founded in 1930 and has been kept alive and vigorous through a continuing string of innovative product concepts. To assure the generation of new ideas and innovative products, the company now offers a systematic course of study based on the Theory of Inventive Problem Solving first developed by Russian inventor Genrikh Altshuller in the late 1940s.

The Invention Leadership Program (ILP) is offered primarily to Motorola's product designers and manufacturing engineers, and has proven effective in reducing development cycles, making designs more reliable, and increasing the pace of idea generation. By following the ILP methodology, participants can more accurately define an engineering problem and, as a result, develop a functional model more quickly.

The ILP is just one of many institutional attempts by Motorola to increase the innovative potential of its global workforce.

The PACE award companies we have studied understand that employees are their best assets. Every company says this, but not all act as if they believe it. PACE winners put this conviction to work, as evidenced in the extent to which they invest in ongoing upgrades in workforce skills. From 1991 to 1995, the average annual hours of training for salaried workers at PACE finalists more than doubled, and it continues to increase, both for salaried and nonsalaried employees. That training is provided in both traditional classroom and computer-based settings. Figure 3.1 indicates the increasing levels of training provided by PACE winners to their salaried and nonsalaried employees.

Dana Corporation not only espouses the importance of its people, but follows through with highly effective programs—Dana University and the company's policy of providing at least 40 hours of education/training to all personnel are the most obvious of these programs. Similar investments in employee capabilities can be found at Motorola, General Electric, McDonald's, Chrysler, and Toyota, all of which have established and maintain ongoing educational operations. Currently, over 1,600 corporate universities are now operating in the United States, up from only 400 a decade earlier.

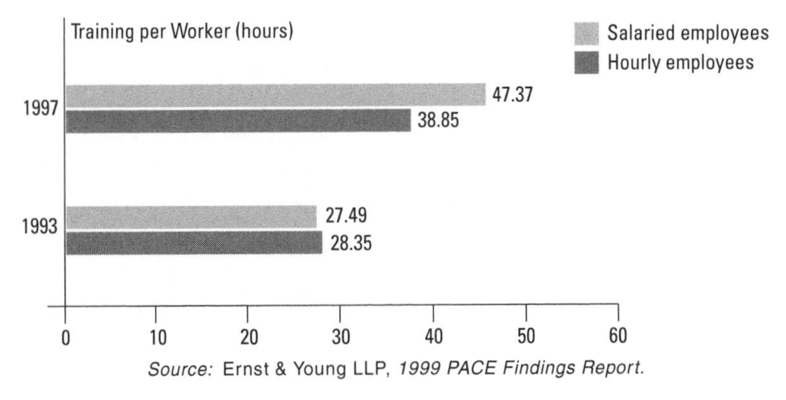

Source: Ernst & Young LLP, *1999 PACE Findings Report.*

Figure 3.1 Training per worker.

Dana University (DU) was founded in 1969, primarily as the outcome of the company's policy of promoting from within. Then-CEO Ren McPherson believed that Dana's internal promotion policy would lead to serious problems unless the company played an active role in educating and training employees to assume higher roles.[2] In addition, DU would teach the "Dana Style" of managing, its corporate culture, values, and policies.

Initially, courses were open to a relatively small percentage of company employees. Over the years, however, these have expanded to include all employees. The first courses were in supervision, and these became the foundation of Dana's current Business School. Courses in cost control soon followed, and a Technical School opened in 1985 with the mission of advancing manufacturing excellence within the company. Realizing that its engineered products had to be properly installed and maintained, DU added a fourth school in 1995 to provide product training to its customers: the Customer and Industrial School.

Today, the company maintains over 70,000 feet of space as classroom and other teaching facilities, operates with a staff over 30 full-time faculty, and boasts an enrollment of almost 6,000 students. Dana is a global corporation with thousands of employees located in Europe, South America, Asia, and other parts of North America, and faculty are maintained in these areas. A growing percentage of DU teaching and training is being conducted off-site.

Many DU courses are recommended by the American Council on Education for college credit and are used by employees seeking associate and undergraduate degrees. In addition, DU's leaders have forged alliances with traditional institutions of higher education. Dana employees can now pursue an MBA degree offered by Bowling Green State University or a master's degree in engineering through the nearby University of Toledo, or an associate's degree in

THE DANA UNIVERSITY SCOREBOARD

Since its founding in 1969, over 49,000 employees have earned supervisor course diplomas and some 3,500 worldwide have become Certified Dana Supervisors through Dana University programs.

manufacturing management from Oakland Community College. The school also partners with the University of Michigan's senior management education program, featuring courses taught by both UM faculty and Dana top management.

Johnson Controls, Inc. (JCI) has sponsored a similar program of continued education for all employees ("Quest"). That program encouraged employees to sign up for management, engineering, and technical courses related to JCI's core technologies. Most were taught in-house on company time either by company experts or by faculty from nearby educational institutions. That program was expanded in 1999 with the formal establishment of the Johnson Controls Institute, a companywide learning organization modeled, in part, on Dana University.

■ A SPIRIT OF EMPLOYEE PARTICIPATION

If your goal is to encourage innovation among rank-and-file employees, logic and experience dictate that those employees have a voice in what gets done and how its done. Employees at Gentex have no trouble finding an audience when they have a new idea. The company has only 1,400 employees (almost entirely in one location), and its executives mingle among them routinely. Management layers are few; the company deliberately keeps these layers to an absolute minimum. Gentex management also gives its blessing to unorthodox reporting relationships, believing that "a little irreverence and rebellion toward traditional corporate structures goes a long way toward lifting the human spirit"[3] and encourages the individual initiative that leads to innovation. The fact that most employees are shareholders also encourages employee participation.

More than most companies we've encountered, Gentex pursues its stated goal of making employees feel and act like entrepreneurs, empowered to innovate and take risks. Its employee ownership policies (described in Chapter 2) support this goal: Gentex people know that they are owners and they act the part.

What is easy and natural at a place like Gentex is much more difficult at a corporation with tens of thousands of employees, many divisions, and soul-deadening bureaucracies. These giant corporations widely recognize the weak pulse of innovation within. Their inability to innovate internally leads them to look outside—to acquisitions and partnerships—for the next wave. There are exceptions: General Electric, Merck, and 3M have shown that bigness is not an absolute deterrent to internal innovation. So too has Dana Corporation. Dana, the third-largest U.S.-based auto/truck supplier, employs more than 86,000 people in dozens of facilities around the world. Yet it manages its operations in a way that these scattered individuals feel their ideas are valued and welcomed. Its antidote to corporate giantism is the *Dana Style.*

➤ The Dana Style

The Dana Style is an operating philosophy that articulates company purpose and its attitude toward employees, suppliers, customers, and quality. It maintains that employees should have the power, desire, tools and opportunity to contribute to the company's success. "It is the total focus and dedication to the human aspect of business," according to corporate Chairman and CEO, Woody Morcott, "as opposed to the purely financial, and it is born out of the notion that business is 90 percent about people and 10 percent about money."[4] This style of management reinforces the belief that individual employees are the true experts when it comes to their specific tasks.

To support its culture of empowered employees, Dana provides personnel development and reward/recognition programs. Dana University, described earlier, is the centerpiece of its approach. The corporation's internal promotion policy is another major building block assuring a reward to those who contribute to the company's success. The "two ideas per month" suggestion program offers additional encouragement; the message is explicit—"We want your ideas."

A decentralized organizational structure probably counts heavily in the Dana Style. In the 1960s, Dana reduced the number of management layers and encouraged employees to supervise themselves. That reduction in management levels resulted in the elimination of 20 inches of policy manuals.

■ OPENING THE FLOW OF INFORMATION

Perhaps nothing creates such a barrier to successful innovation than do organizational structures and practices that constrict the free flow of information or otherwise fail to use it effectively. Information and innovation are practically inseparable, so when you cut off the first, you starve the second.

In the hierarchical organizations that developed in step with the industrial age, information was gathered by middle managers, and passed up to the top. Directives from the top were then relayed downward though the same middle-manager conduits. The whole point of this activity was command and control, not learning and innovation. Those at the top were assumed to *know*. Those at the bottom had one function: to *do*. With the exception of R&D employees, this system put the burden of innovation on the shoulders of senior managers who were generally far removed from direct contact with the outer world of customers, competitors, and new technologies. The rank-and-file employees who *had* direct contact with these factors were not invited to participate in the innovation process. This system failed to make the most of employee potential in many respects, including innovation.

Fewer and fewer companies operate with these outmoded information structures. The trend is away from vertical flows of information and control to others that move information across functional areas of the organization, as shown in Figure 3.2. In the bottom panel of the figure, top-level decision makers continue to be informed and to exercise control through their contacts with the top functional managers, but the functional silos are integrated through information flows that cut horizontally and link all functions with customers and suppliers. In this new model, the flow of information touches many more employees and links them with suppliers and customers.

Most companies use cross-functional teams to overcome some of the drawbacks of their functional organizational structures (see "The LH Platform Team" in Chapter 4). These make it possible to tap into the rich storehouses of expertise found in functional silos, and enlist their support, while avoiding their narrow parochialism.

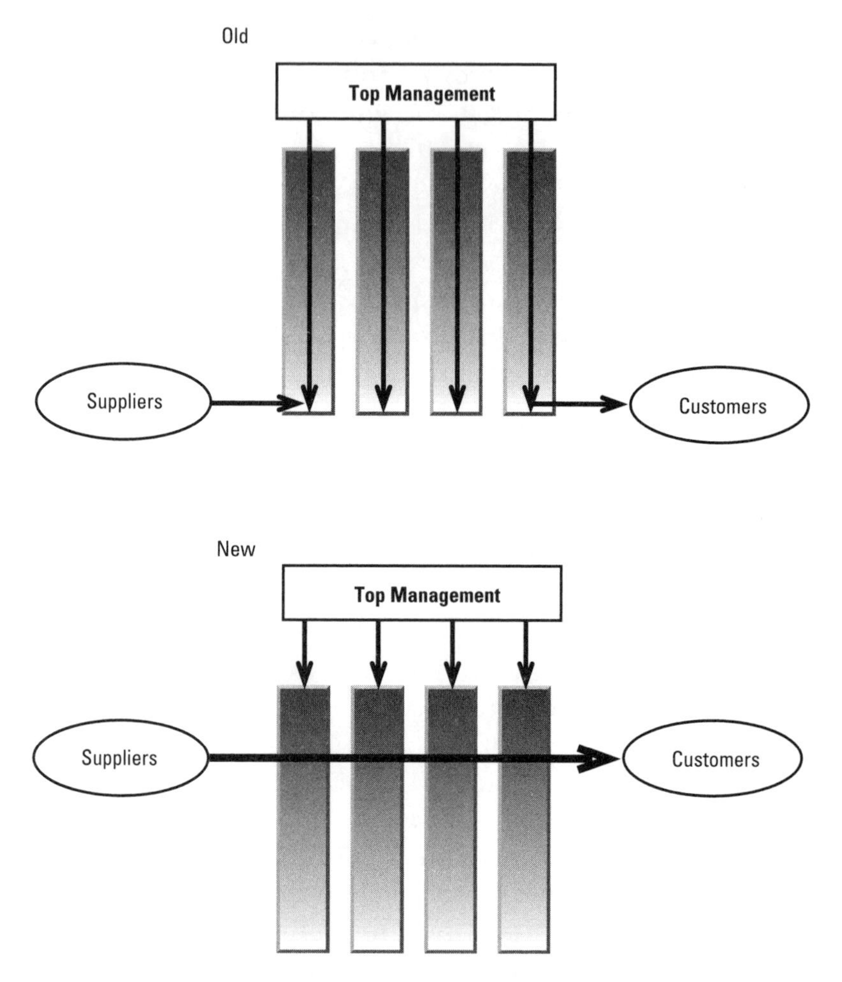

Figure 3.2 The old and new of information flows.

Motorola uses many cross-functional teams, but takes additional steps to encourage the flow of information. At one of our PACE conferences, Brian Wilkie, corporate vice president and general manager of Motorola's Advanced Vehicle Systems Division, described these steps:

➤ *Systematic "repotting" (our term) of individuals from unit to unit over the course of their careers.* This is a great idea for career development, but also serves the ends of information flow, as these individuals pick up and carry technical information, know-how, and observations about best practices from one part of the Motorola universe to another.

➤ *The Scientific Advisor Board Associates (SABA).* Successful innovators are inducted into the SABA, providing opportunities for the cross-pollination of technical ideas from one division to another (e.g., between pagers and cellular phone units).

➤ *Benchmarking exercises.* Like all global enterprises, Motorola must work hard at learning what it already knows. Benchmarking is used internally to move information about best practices from one unit to others.

■ THE COMING BATTLE FOR THE BEST EMPLOYEES

As we enter the twenty-first century, hiring and retaining the *right* people and boosting the capabilities of individual employees will become an even more important challenge. The working populations of Europe, Japan, and the United States are aging, and the pool of potential replacements in the next generation is insufficient for the anticipated level of economic and scientific activity. Paradoxically, the populations with the most favorable ratios of adults to children and adolescents are almost entirely located in Third World nations where education and modern skills are the least developed.

U.S. and Canadian companies have a relative advantage over their European and Japanese competitors in that both benefit enormously from an influx of highly educated and skilled immigrants. Take a stroll through the R&D labs of just about any major U.S. corporation today and in addition to native-born personnel, you'll meet a startling number of scientists and technicians from Europe, Asia, and the Middle East. It is doubtful that you would have this experience anywhere else in the world. These people are not taking jobs from Americans, but are filling vacancies that the country's universities have been unable to satisfy. The demand, in fact, far outstrips supply. In 1999, the U.S. government attempted to alleviate this problem by increasing the number of visas available to technical workers from 65,000 to 115,000. But even this increase failed to meet current needs; less than half-way through the year, almost all these visa positions had been filled.

Immigration notwithstanding, waves of downsizing and years of hiring limits have made the general aging trend at major corporations a serious problem. One senior manager of a major high-tech company, for example, confided recently that years of hiring freezes had boosted the average age of his company's technical/professional workforce to 48 years. That figure was rising at three-quarters of a year annually. "We are not getting enough energetic, young, recently trained people," he worried—and with good reason.

The general aging of populations in the industrial world means that many industries will experience major workforce turnovers in the near future. In the auto industry, for example, an estimated 40 percent of the current workforce will retire by the year 2003. How will these companies attract the people they need to fill their depleted ranks? One way is to create workplaces capable of attracting and retaining skilled and motivated individuals.

Those that do succeed in attracting younger workers find that their new recruits bring different values and skills to the job. Graduates with technical degrees bring new understandings of materials, information science, and management that put them at positions of technical parity if not outright superiority with their older and more experienced coworkers. But these younger hires generally lack the political and social skills that would optimize their effectiveness. An "innovation factory" has to be able to capitalize on the strengths and blunt the weaknesses of these new workers through mentoring and other means.

New Product Development

Development projects provide a comprehensive, real-time test of the systems, structures, and values of the whole organization.

Kent Bowen, Kim Clark, Charles Holloway,
and Steven Wheelwright,
Development Projects: The Engine of Renewal

For most companies, new products (and services) are their most potent generators of growth. According to the *Journal of Product Innovation Management,* companies that exceed the industry average for growth in sales and profitability garner 49 percent of their revenues from *new* products. Those below the industry average draw only 11 percent of revenue from new products.

If you have any doubts about the revenue-generating power of new products, consider what Viagra® has done for Pfizer, what Post-it Notes® has done for 3M, what fiber optics has done for Corning, what its proliferating family of inkjet printers has done for Hewlett-Packard, and what Word®, Excel®, and PowerPoint® have collectively done for Microsoft. In each instance, these products have ignited explosive sales growth and produced tremendous profits. Or look at it from the reverse. What happens when companies fail to launch successful new products? Their current products may continue to sell, but the sales curve eventually flattens as markets become saturated or are invaded by imitators. Prices and margins peak and then tumble. Companies that cannot generate a continuing stream of new and commercially successful products find themselves in a bind, and many turn to acquisitions as a primary growth strategy. Overwhelming evidence from many sources indicates that few acquisitions or mergers create value for shareholders, and some do not even cover their cost of capital.

The only way to sustain revenue and profit growth is through a strategy that brings new offerings to the marketplace at a rate capable of replacing the downward slide of old products, as indicated in Figure 4.1. In this figure, total revenue is the collective revenue contributions of both new and old products. This measure increases as new products are introduced to replace those in decline. For example, the total revenue at time T2 is higher than at T1, even though Product A revenues are on the decline and Product B revenues are flat. Most important, the total revenue slope is headed sharply upward.

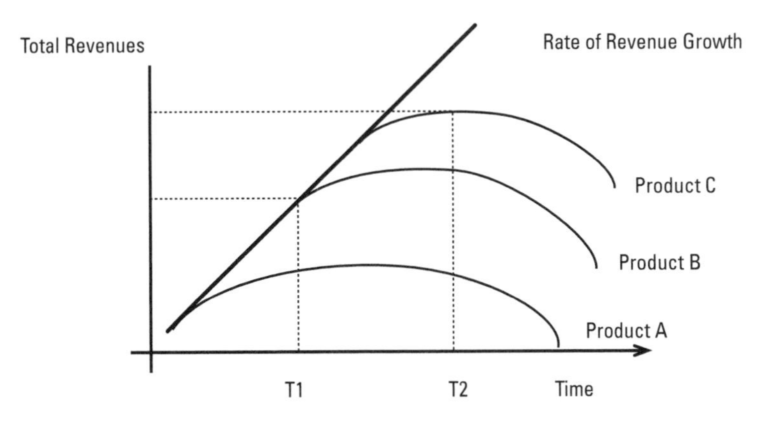

Figure 4.1 Bring new products onstream as old ones fade.

"So," you're thinking, "a continual stream of successful new products is important. That's pretty obvious. But how can we make it happen?"

That's the hard part.

■ USE A PROCESS FOR NEW PRODUCT DEVELOPMENT

Every high-performing company with which we consult attacks the new product problem with some form of new product development (NPD) process that its employees understand and work with on a regular basis. Consider Monroe Auto Equipment, a division of Tenneco. It uses a stage-gate process to evaluate innovative ideas and promote them—or fail them—early. This is the best way to allocate scarce resources, and represents a key competency in the business of new product development.

Robert Cooper, a professor at McMaster University, formally introduced the stage-gate concept in 1990. Cooper studied hundreds of new product development processes and crystallized his observations into the stage-gate idea, which has grown in popularity ever since.[1] The concept itself is simple, and most readers will surely recognize its broader outlines. Less well recognized, however, are the organizational underpinnings that make its implementation successful. Few companies, including some of our PACE winners, have demonstrated an ability to develop those underpinnings.

The stage-gate process shown in Figure 4.2 is a generic version of those used by leading companies. This process has shown itself to be an effective mechanism for converting good ideas into customer-satisfying products. It is something you can manage for:

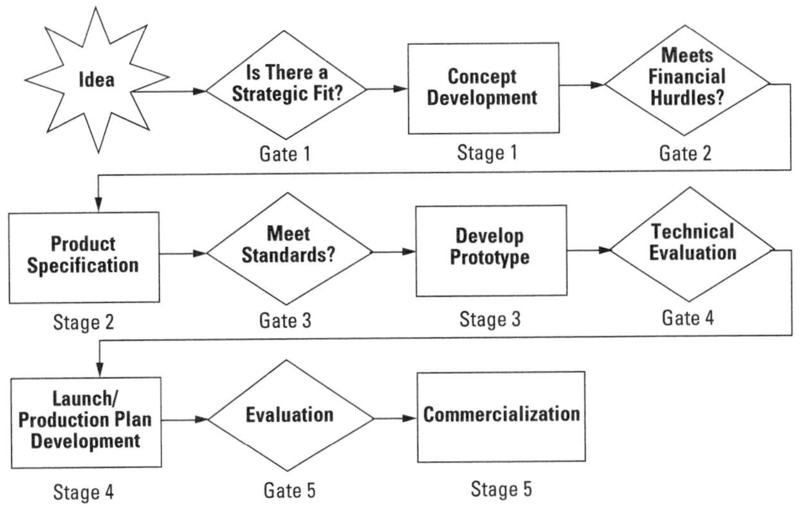

Source: Adapted from Robert G. Cooper, "Stage-Gate Systems: A New Tool for Managing New Products." *Business Horizons,* May–June 1990, 45–54.

Figure 4.2 A generic stage-gate process.

➤ Better quality.

➤ Early elimination of losers.

➤ Faster forward movement of potential winners.

➤ Systematic reduction in technical and market uncertainty.

➤ Acceleration of "time to market."

➤ Replicability.

In the absence of such a process, product development is ad hoc. People with ideas waste lots of time trying to figure out, "How can I get this idea approved and into development?" Likewise, in the absence of a formal process senior managers must reinvent standards for approval and continued funding for each project; the resulting standards are incoherent, arbitrary, or haphazardly applied. Lessons learned in previous development work are left on the shelf and old mistakes are repeated.

Dr. Glenn Omura, PACE judge, tells people to think of each stage in this process as a station where work is done. Each diamond represents a gate at which deliverables can be studied, measured, and checked for quality. As on the factory floor, quality checks must be satisfactory before work can move forward to the next stage.

The first gate in the process, Strategic Fit, evaluates the product idea in terms of corporate competencies and objectives. If somebody has a good idea, we must know if it a good idea for *us*—does the idea fit strategically with our existing

THE CAST OF CHARACTERS

The stage-gate process for product development generally employs two sets of participants. The first group is initially led by the idea generator or the "recognizor" mentioned in Chapter 2. Assuming a favorable reception, a funded project and multifunctional development team form around this initial champion. Together, they perform all the tasks described in the rectangular boxes shown in Figure 4.2. It is important for this team to work effectively together, to have clear roles and responsibilities, to understand how decisions are to be made, and to have executive sponsorship. Team members must feel supported and encouraged by their executive sponsor.

The second group performs the tasks described in the diamond-shaped gates. These teams should be composed of senior managers, with the authority to make decisions and approve continued project funding. Some organizations have a single set of senior managers follow a project through the entire process. Others assign different teams of managers to individual gates. Glenn Omura notes evidence of success with both approaches.

core competencies? Stage 1, Qualitative Evaluation, is something the idea generator or project team must conduct before it can approach the second gate. A market application must be identified and a broad-brush picture of how the idea could be turned into a salable product must be sketched out. At Gate 2, the merits of this qualitative evaluation are judged and, if given a green light, the idea moves forward to the next stage of development.

Gates control the development process just as quality control controls the manufacturing process. Each gate measures how well the project stands up to one or another standard: strategic, market, financial, or technical. Those that pass are hustled forward. Those that do not are either killed or cycled back to an earlier stage for more development.

The stage-gate system has a big benefit: like every work process, it is *replicable* and *improvable.* This is critically important for organizations when innovation and new product development occur with regularity, and may it explain why organizations that use a formal process get their new products to market faster than those that do not.

■ THE NPD PROCESS IN ACTION

The Construction Products Division of W.R. Grace, Inc., is a half-billion-dollar global business with three major lines: additives designed to modify cement-based materials for durability, strength, and placement properties; materials that protect structural steel from fire; and waterproofing membranes. Development of new products is a key part of its strategy for growth, according to Felek Jachimowicz, Vice President of Research and Technology.

Jachimowicz and his colleagues rely heavily on a stage-gate product development process (PDP) to assure the orderly development and commercialization of the many ideas conceived in the division's R&D labs and through market research and contacts with customers. As described by Jachimowicz:

> *We use it for a number of things: as a major communications vehicle between different functions, and as an integration vehicle between different functions—technical, marketing, engineering, and so forth. We also use it as a tool for monitoring progress and for making adjustments. And, last but not least, we use the PDP as a learning device—as a way of spreading best practices across all product lines.*

Grace Construction's product development process is an adaptation of Robert Cooper's stage-gate system and was first implemented in the mid-1990s. Projects that enter the PDP must pass through review and decision points staffed by personnel of an "appropriate level," the aim being to use reviewers and decision makers closest to the action. The division's flat organization facilitates this flexibility. "[In this division] everybody knows about everything," says Jachimowicz, "from the general manager to individual researchers. Communications are very open and unfiltered." Typically, both he and the general manager act as stage-gate reviewers, along with key marketing and technical personnel.

The path through Grace's PDP is often bumpy. Some projects fail in their first attempts to pass through a gate and are sent back for more work. Others are killed entirely, in most cases because: (1) they cannot meet technical performance targets, and (2) the opportunity visualized at the project's inception has become less attractive.

Grace Construction Products has found that its PDP has made product development more disciplined, more transparent, and more accountable, and its continued use has led to several adaptations as division personnel have gained experience in using it. "The challenge is to use it in a constructive way," notes Jachimowicz, "and not allow it to be corrupted into a bureaucratic thing."

Many companies use a process similar to the one employed by Grace Construction Products, including Exxon,

ANALYTICAL TOOLS

Most companies apply quantitative tools at appropriate gates: net present value (NPV) and internal rate of return (IRR) analysis based on pro forma cash flow statements; breakeven analysis; and decision tree, sensitivity, and probability analysis.* In general, these tools attempt to estimate the future financial value of the technology or product under development. The utility of these tools, however, depends on the reliability of quantitative forecasts and on the objective application of the tools themselves.

These tools are of minimal value in the very early project stages, according to most sources, but become more effective as uncertainty with respect to costs, pricing, and sales projections is reduced. What companies need most in the early stages, cautions Felek Jachimowicz, is not a set of analytical tools but a good strategic assessment of the opportunity. The substantial risks that inevitably surround an early-stage project require an opportunity that is correspondingly high. Some companies have quantitative hurdles that any opportunity must measure up to (e.g., "the project must have the potential of producing $50 million in additional revenue within 3 years of launch"), Grace Construction Products uses a qualitative hurdle: a new project must have the potential "to make a significant difference."

---

* For a complete treatment of analytical valuation techniques, see F. Peter Boer, *The Valuation of Technology: Business and Financial Issues in R&D* (New York: John Wiley & Sons, 1999).

3M, IBM, General Motors, and Johnson Controls. Some, especially those that are very marketing oriented, put a greater emphasis on the front end of the process, trying to match up product definition with what the market really wants. As described by PACE judge Glenn Omura, "They start with a very sharp product definition before they go forward."

Most evidence supports Felek Jachimowicz's observation about the organizational benefits of developing a good process and giving people opportunities to work through it. For example, the GM employees who use that company's four-step process have told Glenn Omura:

> *. . . it creates a common process throughout the entire organization. This common process leads to common measures, practices, and systems. Commonness does not drum out creativity, but rather . . . takes the best practices and feeds them to the other divisions. The result, they claim, is that they get a set of best practices that reduces cycle time . . . It leads to discipline [and] builds the right kind of culture.*[2]

■ WHAT A PROCESS CANNOT DO

The stage-gate or other NPD process is highly useful, but cannot solve all your new product problems:

➤ *It cannot generate ideas.* High-value ideas must be generated *outside* the process. Unless a company is capable of generating commercially promising ideas on a regular basis, a new product development process—in any form—will be only so much window dressing to review and push along incremental product innovations. Grace Construction Products has attempted to remedy this problem by appending a "Technology Building Process" at the fuzzy front end of its PDP. This process acts as a feeding mechanism for the PDP, nurturing promising ideas and bringing them up to a point where they can enter the stage-gate PDP with reasonable confidence of success. Generally, idea nurturing means defining technical ideas in substantial detail and identifying market applications.

It is essential to have many ideas entering the process, and to use good filters for killing the bad ones.

There is also evidence that a stage-gate or other formal process is ill-suited to early stage projects of *radical* innovation. These early-stage projects simply cannot answer the specific questions asked at various gates, and the imposition of such a process too early is likely to kill good ideas better left alone in the idea incubator. As Glenn Omura has told us, "If it's a soft, fuzzy idea, it's difficult to have a systematic organizational process usher it toward implementation."

➤ *It cannot turn lemons into lemonade.* The collaboration of project and decision teams can make good ideas better, but cannot make good ideas out of bad ones. Authors James and David Matheson have described an R&D "dialogue process" that augments current ideas with various alternatives; this process, they say, almost always leads to better outcomes.[3] However, this process, like Grace's Technology Building Process, operates at the fuzzy front end of product development—not within the development process itself. We've seen no example of lame ideas being turned into powerful ones with the stage-gate process.

➤ *It does not solve the larger problem of prioritization and portfolio management.* A NPD process considers only one project at a time. It does not address the strategic challenge of creating a balanced portfolio of high-risk breakthrough and moderate risk incremental projects. Nor does it tell decision makers where to invest limited R&D resources.

■ PLATFORM POWER

No chapter on new product development would be complete without some discussion of product platforms and their development. As defined by Marc Meyer and Al Lehnerd, a product platform is "a set of subsystems and interfaces that form a common structure from which a stream of derivative products can be efficiently developed and produced."[4] Auto makers have used the platform concept for decades, though not always particularly well.

Powerful product platforms are found in many product categories and have created substantial wealth for their corporate innovators: the core technology of the HP inkjet printer; the innards of the Swatch Watch from which hundreds of unique designs have emerged; the electric motors that power Black & Decker hand tools, and so on. Each has at its core a simple but elegantly designed set of components and interfaces that collectively support a broad family of related products, each member of which is designed for a minimum incremental cost to target a particular market niche. While their competitors develop and commercialize one product at a time, companies that focus their resources on a basic platform aim to create an entire portfolio of products that maximize the benefits of common components and design for manufacturability.

Once a platform is developed and successfully tested, it becomes the launching pad for dozens of derivative products with new and unique performance features. These derivative products provide sales momentum for the product family and opportunities to introduce technical enhancements. The wise company uses this period of growth to develop a new generation product platform based on leading-edge technology, as shown in Figure 4.3. Products from the second generation platform render those of the first obsolete.

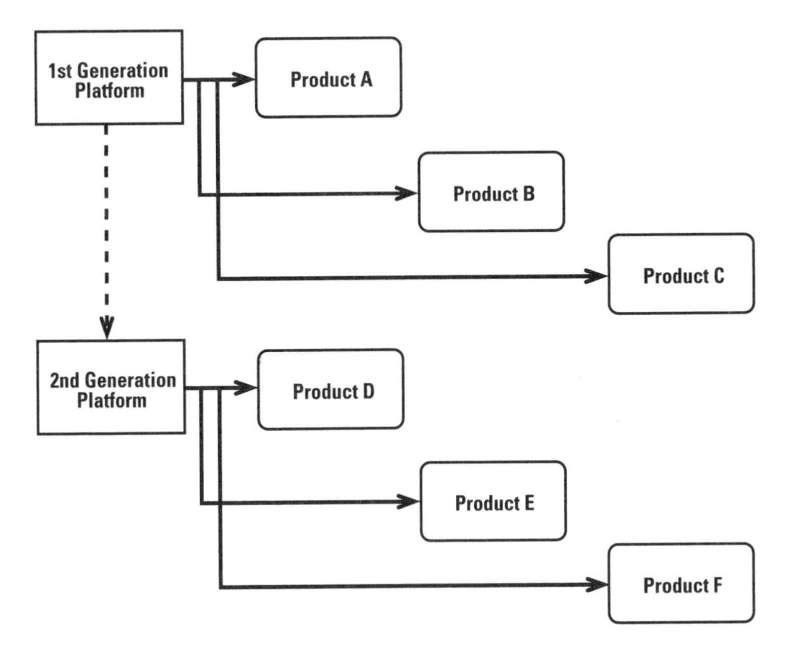

Figure 4.3 Succeeding generations of product platforms and their families.

Toyota is very effective at the reuse of parts and achieves 60 percent carryover of parts from one generation or model to the next. This has obvious benefits: less capital required for tooling, fixtures, and process revision. The risk of quality degradation with the launch of the new product is minimized or eliminated. Finally, the launch process itself is faster and more effective.

At Motorola's Advanced Vehicle Systems Division, Brian Wilkie applies the terms "reuse" and "modularity" to describe his own company's approach to designing and developing platforms. Motorola engineers are taught to think about how things designed for one application can be reused in others. "Several generations of engine controllers used in the U.S. auto market," he explained in an interview, "use the same central processing unit used in the PalmPilot and various generations of cell phone." By designing application *robustness* into their electronics, Motorola engineers leverage their output among many, often unrelated, products and product categories. This cuts overall development time and produces a much higher return on investments. Some of that return is shared with the engineers. "At Motorola," said Wilkie, "when we give an award for an innovation, we also give an award to the person who has found a way to reuse it."

By combining the development of derivative products with the creation of new generations of its product platform, a company is assured a steady stream of revenue from new products even as it renews its core technology.

■ THE SUPPLIER ROLE

The role of suppliers in new product development is growing in many industries. Successful suppliers don't just sit on their hands waiting for their OEM customers to describe design specs. Instead, they get out ahead of their OEMs and learn directly what their customers' customers would view favorably. Great suppliers gain market insight and equip themselves with the R&D wherewithal to spearhead product innovation.

As shown in Figure 4.4, our PACE finalists have assumed more of the product design responsibilities once reserved to OEMs as those OEMs place more faith in their technical capabilities. Half the products supplied by PACE finalists in recent years have been "black box" designs—a good example being Goodyear's "run flat" tire. Other than general operating specifications, these required little or no design work by OEMs. One-third of supplier products resulted from joint development efforts, or so-called "gray box" development. The balance were products built completely to OEM specifications.

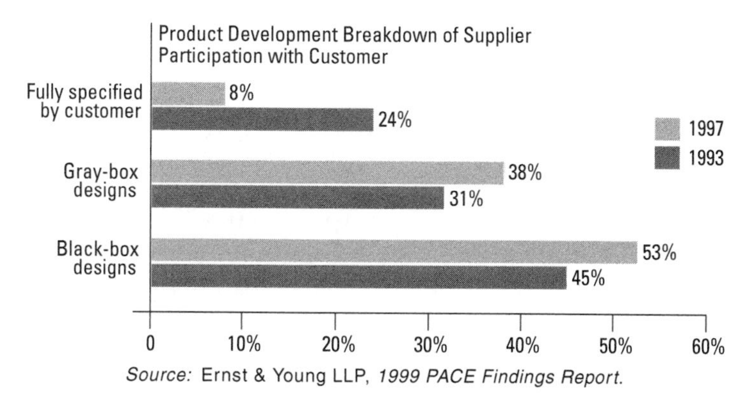

Figure 4.4 PACE supplier role in new product development.

■ TOWARD GREATER SPEED AND EFFICIENCY

If the auto industry is a harbinger of things to come, the ability to develop new products quickly and efficiently will surely become more important as time passes. A study sponsored by Ernst & Young and conducted by the University of Michigan's Transportation Research Institute has predicted that between 1998 and 2007 auto makers will reduce the amount of time it takes to design a new vehicle by one-third.[5] This means reducing vehicle development time from the 1998 range of 30 to 38 months to 20 to 26 months in 2007. To accomplish this time reduction, vehicle manufactures and their suppliers will have to make greater use of technologies and work processes that have proven effective in maintaining development quality as time-to-market is cut:

- Computer aid design and modeling.
- Computer simulations.
- Virtual prototyping.
- NPD processes like the ones described above.

- More effective collaboration between OEMs and suppliers.

In the PACE Awards program, we see that winners don't merely use such approaches, they make them *central competencies*. Consequently, these companies have shorter product development cycle times and expanded "what if" capabilities. They are more effective at identifying and assessing trade-offs during the design and engineering phases. To survive and prosper in the years ahead, every company will have to become more effective in the business of new product development.

And there is plenty of room for improvement. The U.S. auto industry collectively spends an estimated $400–$500 million each year on product teardown and analysis. Teams of engineers at GM, for instance, will purchase and disassemble a Toyota Camry, analyze its design, its key systems and individual components, and make inferences about its production process and estimated production time. Meanwhile, engineers at Ford, Honda, DaimlerChrysler, Nissan, and other car makers will be doing the same thing. Tier One suppliers to these companies are doing the same. This work is not only expensive and redundant, but adds at least a week to new vehicle development schedules.

Vehicle teardown represents one of many opportunities to take time and cost out of the new product cycle. Conceivably, either an independent enterprise or an industry consortium could do the same teardown and analysis *once* and make the information available to subscribers or consortium members at a fraction of the cost in dollars and development time.

➤ Optimizing Development Activities

There is also the daunting problem of optimizing the allocation of scarce development resources: namely, people and

WHY TIME MATTERS

Everyone understands that long product development cycles add to costs and delay the receipt of revenues, reducing the present value of cash flow from new product sales. The current long lead times experienced by auto makers and manufacturers of other complex assembled products create two other serious problems:

1. *The longer the lead time, the less likely we are to match our designs with future customer tastes and requirements.* For example, if we begin design work on a new vehicle based on customer research conducted in 1999, customer tastes and requirements are likely to change to some degree by the time the vehicle is launched in 2002. The longer the development cycle, the greater the problem.
2. *Long lead times can lock old technologies into the design.* We want to assure that technologies designed into our new product designs are still leading edge technologies when those products are launched. This is extremely difficult when lead times are 3 to 4 years and gives short-cycle manufacturers a big advantage with customers. In the auto business, the U.S. auto maker whose new model hits the streets in 2002 will be based on 1998 or 1999 technologies; the typical Japanese new model launched in 2002, in contrast, will be based on 1999 or 2000 technology.

equipment. An NPD process can inform management which projects should move forward, which need more work, and which should be canceled. It can*not,* however, assure that resources are properly allocated between active development projects. This problem is especially acute when companies have 20 to 30 active projects scattered across the product development cycle. A stage-gate system can help us understand

and manage these individual projects, but is of no help in managing their sum total.

We need a way to aggregate these projects and balance their demands for resources against available resources and against company priorities. Currently, few companies do this well. They rely on manual systems and fail to look at demand across programs. Software tools to deal with this problem are now available, and their dexerity is bound to increase in the years ahead. For example, i2 Technologies of Dallas, Texas, provides an extensive suite of software tools to handle NPD resource and project management, including portfolio planning, constraint-based project management, and the synchronizing of launch planning with the supply chain. The tools themselves are built around the principles of Theory-of-Constraints (TOC), and leverage memory-resident calculation for very rapid scenario evaluation and optimization. Compared with traditional manual methods, or semimanual simple desktop systems, these tools make it possible for companies to dynamically optimize product portfolios while recognizing critical constraints in engineering personnel, equipment, or the supply chain. Development portfolios and project schedules can be optimized for multiple financial objectives, for accelerated time-to-market, or for increased development pipeline throughput. i2's solutions also enable real-time Web-based links among development partners and suppliers, making design changes faster and easier. It is expected that such capabilities will become more and more critical as OEMs off-load larger percentages of their product development to their key suppliers.

➤ Data Integration

Developers of complex products can also save time and money through the integration of the materials and scheduling software. Databases that contain part lists and part revision levels should be integrated with other databases that contain information about the dimensions and characteristics of these parts, inventory, scheduling and so on, and all should be integrated with the corporate Enterprise Resource Planning (ERP) system software. This assures that newly designed parts enter the materials management system and that time-wasting mistakes do not add days or weeks to development schedules; it also eliminates the risk that someone will be ordering a part that is already being phased out in favor of an improved version.

➤ Postponement

Some companies are learning to speed up new product introductions by what Hewlett-Packard calls "postponement," a technique that adds the differentiating features of a new product at the latest possible stage in the manufacturing or assembly process. This approach goes hand-in-glove with the platform strategy described earlier. Here, the manufacturer can build-to-stock the core elements of any one of a number of products—elements that are essentially transparent to the customers. Development teams then design unique performance features or product characteristics that are added to the common platform in the final stages of manufacturing. Postponement greatly reduces time and effort in both product development and retooling in the manufacturing plant. In effect, this is how HP has been able to introduce so many versions of its inkjet printers so rapidly. It is also what Societé Micromécanique et Horlogère (SMH), Switzerland's largest watchmaker, did in the 1980s to recover markets lost earlier to Asian imports. Once it had developed an inexpensive but reliable quartz timekeeping core, the company could roll out a continuing stream of attractive and unique watches under the Swatch label. All the unique features of these fashionable timepieces were added at the end of the development and assembly process. What customers saw, however, was an entirely new and unique watch.[6]

➤ Colocation

Fred Bauer of Gentex spoke to the importance of colocating product developers and manufacturers earlier in this book. Nevertheless, companies continue to fail to bring product developers and manufacturing personnel into physical or communications proximity. This failure inevitably leads to mistakes and misunderstandings and adds days if not months to the development cycle.

➤ Expectations

Sometimes, long development cycles are abetted by the expectations of operating personnel and their managers. If they have always taken three months to do something, and if three months is the time typically allotted in the schedule, people will testify, "It takes three months to complete that job." Necessity is often the best antidote to these expectations, as the following story confirms.

During the early months of the war in the Pacific, the U.S. naval command at Pearl Harbor was hurriedly assembling a carrier task force to intercept a much larger Japanese invasion fleet steaming at the time toward Midway Island, a critical communications and fueling point halfway between the Pearl Harbor and the Japanese home islands. The U.S. task force needed all the firepower it could muster, but one of its three designated carriers was a doubtful participant. The *USS Yorktown* had just limped in from the Battle of the Coral Sea with heavy bomb damage, and naval engineers estimated that she would need at least 90 days in dry dock to be make fit for duty. Because the war would not stop for 90 days, repair crews worked round the clock to rehabilitate the damaged ship. Three days later, with welders and electricians still working feverishly beneath her flight deck, *Yorktown* was piloted out of Pearl Harbor toward the most decisive naval engagement of the war.

People can do remarkable things when necessity demands it. In the industrial sector, consider DaimlerChrysler's experience with developing the tooling for one model year's new engine hood. Historically, the company allowed for 32 weeks in its schedule for the design and production of the tooling for the inner and outer hood pieces. One year, a problem with the hood tooling was discovered very near the scheduled launched date of the vehicle. New tooling would have to be built and tested before a single vehicle could be put through assembly. Delaying model launch by 32 weeks was clearly unthinkable. Like the crews that repaired the *Yorktown,* DC's tooling team attacked the problem with a must-do attitude and a renewed spirit of collaboration, producing and satisfactorily testing new hood tooling in just 208 hours![7]

■ TEAMS

Individuals are almost always the source of important new ideas. That holds true for new product concepts as well. However, moving an idea through development to launch requires a level of resources that only an organization of many individuals can muster. And the experience of the past 20 years indicates that a dedicated product team is almost always the best approach to getting things done quickly, at the least cost, and with the best result:

➤ *The IBM PC.* When IBM got serious about the personal computer business around 1980, it knew that any attempt to design so innovative a product through its normal channels, which were dominated by IBM's mainframe culture, would be the kiss of death. So it set up a remote skunkworks in Boca Raton, Florida, staffed it with a small number of its best engineers, and gave it plenty of decision-making freedom. Within a very short time, that team created a design that defined personal computing for years to come.

➤ *Team Zebra.* During the mid-1980s, Kodak's black-and-white film business found itself beleaguered in a market it had owned for a century. It fought back successfully, thanks to a dedicated team of technical, manufacturing, and marketing personnel.

➤ *Reengineering of customer response at Polaroid.* Cambridge-based Polaroid Corporation faced serious challenges during the early 1990s. Its sales were flat; technology was rapidly changing, and the mass merchandisers that distributed most of the company's consumer products were demanding much higher levels of supplier performance than Polaroid could deliver. One of its responses was total reengineering of North American customer fulfillment, led by a cross-functional team of dedicated employees. In less than two years, this team total revamped and reinvigorated Polaroid's customer connection.

➤ The LH Platform Team

It's likely that every industry can relate a spectacular team performance such as those just cited. In our own industry, the Chrysler LH Platform team led by now-retired executive Glenn Gardner is both legendary and full of practical lessons about what teams can do and how they should operate. (Glenn was also the leader of the 50-person team that produced the revolutionary Chrysler "minivan.")

The LH team was responsible for developing and launching the innovative "cab forward" design now used in many popular DaimlerChrysler models. Aside from the market acceptance of LH platform vehicles, the most striking thing about the development effort was the team's success in slashing development time and costs. The first LH vehicle rolled off the assembly line approximately 39 months from the project's inception (versus Chrysler's then-typical 60 months), and accomplished its task using only *half* the number of personnel and only two-thirds the investment dedicated to equivalent new vehicle projects. These vehicles also achieved higher quality scores than had any other Chrysler products.

The LH platform team achieved what every CEO prays for: *faster, less costly,* and *better!* When we asked Glenn Gardner to share his insights about how his team produced these results, he cited four things:

1. *A clear, single goal.* People who work in a functional environment have dozens of responsibilities: ongoing operations, budgets, performance reviews, and so forth. These activities dilute the ability of even extraordinary people to produce breakthrough results. This can be avoided if team members are charged with focused objectives.
2. *The boss's public endorsement of the team's goal and its plan to achieve it.* Gardner's LH team got then-CEO Robert Lutz to meet with it every 6 to 8 weeks to review progress and reaffirm top-level support. Vice presidents of all line organizations were invited and encouraged to attend; their presence cleared the air of the unproductive speculation that typically surrounds team projects, and diffused the potential for disagreements. "It kept people from coming around the backside to undercut the team," according to Gardner. Further, vetting information with these VP

prior to meetings with the CEO helped to avoid surprises and to build trust between the team and the functional units whose support they needed. Lutz's public communication with the rest of the company about the team's work and its importance to the entire corporation helped clear away internal barriers to progress.

3. *Excellent and ongoing communications with the rest of the company.* "The team has a responsibility to communicate what it is doing—and how—to the functional groups." According to Gardner, the resources and executive attention showered on major project teams can inspire resentment among other employees, who keep the wheels of the company turning without fanfare. "In the eyes of some, [team members] are prima donnas." To avoid this unhealthy situation, Gardner recommends that technical specialists on the team (e.g., brake specialists, marketers, electric systems specialists) act as emissaries to the community of related specialists. The DaimlerChrysler informal "Tech Clubs" were an outcome of this advice. Each emissary is charged with keeping his or her technical compatriots in the company informed on the progress and problems experienced by the team, and with enlisting their ideas and support. The Tech Clubs and Project Team Communications are excellent potential applications of e-Commerce and Knowledge Repositories. Being able to obtain and manage knowledge across platform teams, exchange design and test information, search for new material, and include the extended enterprise offers great potential for reducing product development time and cost.

4. *Core team members remained involved in the project through launch and commercialization.* Gardner learned

the hard way how the integrity of a great project can be threatened once it is released to functional groups outside the development loop. "With the original minivan we had everything done except the detail releases," Gardner recollected.

> *We turned it over to engineering to do the detail releasing. Then our team of 50 people ran around the company trying to make sure they didn't screw it up. . . . Once it got into the big system, everyone thought he had a better idea, or told us 'you can't do that.' Luckily, the company was in such big trouble at the time than no one wanted a big battle—so we won most of the fights. Even so, they slipped in more than a few changes without our knowing about it. . . . You'd be out driving a prototype and there they'd be.*

Gardner and his team didn't allow this to happen with the LH project. Instead of handing of the project for final development and manufacturing, a core group stayed on to provide advice, oversight, and to protect the integrity of the design the team had worked so hard to create and develop.

■ PRODUCT DEVELOPMENT AS LEARNING LAB

New product development is, in a real sense, a laboratory for learning and renewal for the entire organization. Engineers, designers, marketing and manufacturing specialists, and managers from other functions come together in this laboratory and, together, engage the future. Engaging the future means developing better understanding of customers and markets, and developing new skills, new knowledge, and new ways of organizing for speed, cost reduction, and customer satisfaction. Ideally, these new capabilities will be diffused from product development to other areas of the company.

As described by a team of academics that researched development projects in many settings:

> *Without exception, the most successful projects [we] examined were those in which the teams operated in learning environment. People learned from previous projects, advanced their skills during the course of the project, and applied what they learned to renew the company's capabilities.*[8]

Thus, the goal of product development should not be solely the commercialization of new products. Organizational learning and renewing are equally important. Development teams should learn from their mistakes and from their successes. Ask yourself:

- ➤ Does your company conduct postmortems on completed projects?
- ➤ Are successful experiments with new forms of cross-functional teamwork deliberately replicated elsewhere in the organization?
- ➤ Are your engineers and technical personnel acquiring new skills and knowledge?
- ➤ Is the process of development becoming progressively better understood and more effective?

These are the questions that every manager should ask about his or her company's NPD efforts.

The Power of Process Innovation

Product development enjoys an early wave of innovation, but its rate subsidies and gives way to a growing rate of process innovation.

James M. Utterback
Mastering the Dynamics of Innovation

People with no industrial background generally view innovation narrowly, as a breakthrough product like the flat screen display that makes laptop computers possible. Our homes and offices are filled with product innovations that make life easier, more interesting, or just plain different. Self-cleaning ovens, cell phones, heart pacemakers, transdermal patches, inkjet printers, breadmakers, and goof-proof fully automated cameras. The list is practically endless. Beneath the surface of the world of innovative *things,* however, is a less visible world of innovative *processes.* Many of the *things* we find useful today would not exist, or would be unaffordable, were it not for these processes.

Forty years ago, plate glass—now used in automobiles, commercial building sheathing, mirrors, glass doors, and hundreds of other applications—was manufactured through a laborious and costly set of disconnected procedures that began with melting raw materials, casting the liquid glass, and heating it in an annealing oven. Once an individual casting cooled, it had to be ground and polished by huge machines using lots of abrasives and polishing materials. Thanks to innovations achieved in the 1960s by Britain's Pilkington Glass, that long and costly set of steps has been reduced to a continuous flow process, making plate glass plentiful and relatively cheap. Equally notable examples are found in the fields of textiles, petroleum products, plastics, and coatings.

The power of process innovation to shift the balance of cost and quality leadership has been demonstrated through the decades and across industries. Nucor Corporation, the mini-mill steelmaker, didn't break into the ranks of major steel producers in the usual way (i.e., with hugely capitalized mills and fleets of ore boats). Hardly. Much of Nucor's current success can be traced directly to its 1986 introduction of continuous casting, a process that had eluded generations of steel men. This innovative process, which it purchased from a German engineering firm for what now seems a pittance, eliminated most of the arduous and capital-intensive steps used by traditional steelmakers. Instead of casting a mattress-size slab of white-hot steel and progressively reducing its thickness through a mile-long series of milling and reheating steps, Nucor's radical new process cast a thin ribbon of steel that could be directly milled, cut, and shipped. Nucor, like every process innovator, took major risks in developing its new and revolutionary methods, but those risks paid off in cost leadership.

No discussion of process innovation would be complete without a reference to Toyota Motor Company, which has been a leader in process innovation over the past 20 years. That author's first exposure to the Toyota Production System (TPS) occurred in the late 1970s as production control supervisor responsible for five departments making stampings, injection molded parts, and machined parts. We had all heard the claims made for TPS, but these seemed highly questionable, given our experience. Level production scheduling was a dream. The *kanban* system and perfect quality sounded like wishful thinking. Changeover time measured in minutes instead of the usual hours or days was out of the question. We were committed to running large lot quantities for days at a time. And why not? Nobody ever yelled at us for producing too much inventory. But shut down the assembly line—for any reason—and the general manager would put a black mark by your name.

Toyota's results in the marketplace, however, proved that process matters, and turned doubters (like the author) into believers. Many U.S. manufacturers soon began learning the lessons of TPS, reforming their processes for administrative, financial, selling, and product development.

THE RELATIONSHIP BETWEEN PRODUCT AND PROCESS INNOVATIONS

The work of two scholars has helped us to understand the relationship between product and process innovation. MIT's James Utterback has observed that "product development enjoys an early wave of innovation, but that rate subsides and gives way to a growing rate of process innovation."* Once a product design is established, people's energies are channeled into finding better ways of producing it.

The research of Robert Stobaugh of Harvard Business School, on the other hand, indicates that the pace of *major* process innovations progressively drops off as the product ages, as shown in Figure 5.1.

* James M. Utterback, *Mastering the Dynamics of Innovation* (Boston, MA: Harvard Business School Publishing, 1994), 126.

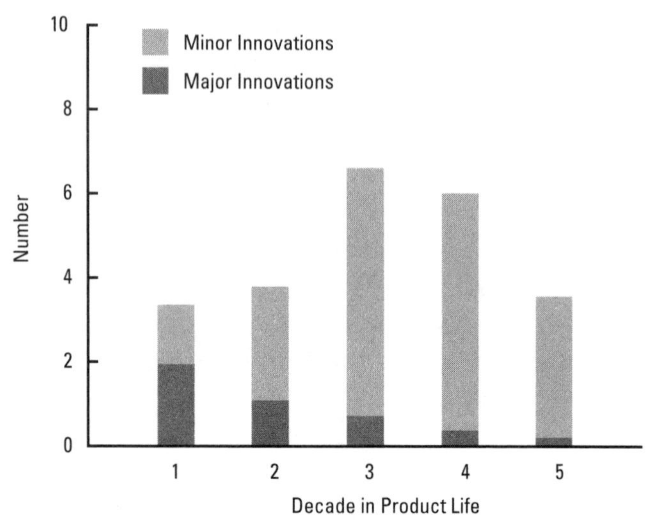

Source: Robert Stobaugh, *Innovation and Competition: The Global Management of Petrochemical Products* (Boston: Harvard Business School Press, 1988), p. 26. Used with permission.

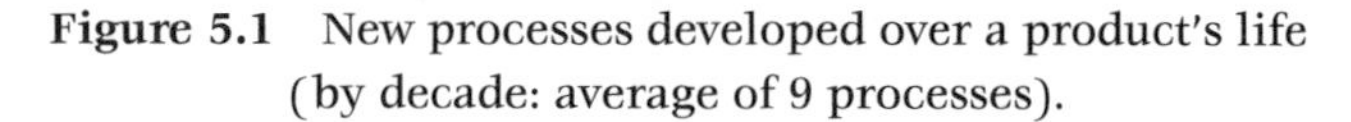

Figure 5.1 New processes developed over a product's life (by decade: average of 9 processes).

■ PROCESS INNOVATION AND COMPETITIVE EXCELLENCE

Excellent companies are always improving their manufacturing and business processes with the goal of achieving greater efficiency, quality, and flexibility. The results are not hard to find. Consider quality. In just four years, our PACE finalists cut customer defect notices and final inspection defects by more than 50 percent. Rework and scrap rates likewise improved. For example, Monroe Auto Equipment Company (a division of Tenneco Automotive) redesigned a painting process that involved numerous steps and the handling of many hazardous waste-producing materials. Thanks to process innovations, Monroe now has a cleaner chemical paint process that bonds paint polymers directly to exposed iron surfaces. The application, which allows the painting of shock absorber bodies, completely revamped Monroe's traditional painting process for underbody componentry, reaching new levels of precision and durability while leaving shock absorber rods unaffected. The process works without high-temperature curing, effectively reducing cycle time, energy costs, and potentially harmful emissions. Monroe has applied this process innovation throughout its applicable operations in North America and overseas.

Leading companies are taking new approaches to their processes, including the placement of some engineers in marketing and customer contact positions. We found that only 23 percent of engineers working for PACE Award winners were located in their own areas, compared with 69 percent just five years earlier. Sixty-nine percent of these engineers reported being located with or near customers compared with 31 percent five years earlier.

The best companies look at process innovation both tactically and strategically. They understand that process innovation will enhance cost and time savings and lead to higher quality in current operations, but they also see strategic benefits from learning how to play by new rules. In 1995, the Parish Light Vehicle Structure Division of Dana Corporation became the first North American frame supplier to Toyota, the world's most efficient maker of automobiles. Claiming that honor was no small feat, given Toyota's Olympian standards of supplier performance. Dana understood that the difficult and costly effort to win this coveted status would pay big dividends for its Parish Division; but it also understood that the know-how gained by playing in the same league with Toyota could be leverage across its divisions to the betterment of each. This, in fact, is what has happened, and a combination of process innovations and improvements at the Parish frame plant in

Stockton, California, opened the door to new business and new customer relationships for Dana. Start-up investments were high, but they paid off.

Today, some 240 Parish employees build up to 700 vehicle frames each day at a 100,000-square-foot facility in Stockton, California. In 1998 alone, the plant shipped 158,000 thousand frames to the NUMMI (New United Motor Manufacturing Inc.) plant in nearby Fremont where they are assembled into many models of the popular Toyota Tacoma compact pickup truck. The Parish frame plant was built in 1995 exclusively for this purpose and was the first facility in North America capable of meeting Toyota's stringent just-in-time, just-in-sequence standards. In addition to state-of-the-art robotic assembly and paint systems, the Parish plant is equipped with redundant systems to prevent unanticipated outages at its facility from disrupting production at the NUMMI assembly plant. The production process itself was jointly designed and planned by Dana and Toyota.

The level of process sophistication in Parish's plant is evidenced by its ability to make line changeover in just 7 seconds for any of the 10 Toyota frame models it produces (in line with Toyota's "single minute changeover" requirements). This makes it possible to economically build frames in lot sizes of one, and to provide frame models in the *exact order* required by NUMMI. This flexibility and speed is required, since NUMMI operates under the Toyota production system, which only builds in response to customer orders—a "customer-pull" operation. Each vehicle coming down NUMMI's Tacoma line is different—a different model, a different color, a different engine size, and so on—and each supplier must deliver its components in that exact order. This system of "mass customization" stands in stark contrast to the production practices of the U.S. Big Three, which continue to operate on a "supply-push" concept that runs 500 or more identical models down a line before making a changeover.

There is little or no margin for error for suppliers in the production system just described. Says plant manager Dan Cavanaugh, "The process has no buffers, no safety stocks." Every item must be the right item, built error-free, sequenced in the right delivery order, and delivered just in time. So, flatbed trucks will typically pick up Parish frames every two hours during the typical day and deliver them to the NUMMI production line. Few suppliers can operate at this level of process perfection. According to Cavanaugh, "It's a tough commitment. The just-in-time Toyota production system tests your courage."

■ THE PRODUCT-PROCESS CONNECTION

When Fred Bauer talks about the electrochromic technology developed by Gentex scientists and engineers, he talks about manufacturing process innovations in the next breath. The two often go hand in hand. In fact, it is rare to find a truly revolutionary product innovation that can be produced effectively through existing processes. For example, the aspheric exterior mirrors Gentex introduced in 1997 incorporate Night Vision Safety™ (NVS) technology and provide nearly three times the vision field of traditional flat exterior mirrors. These mirrors are a big hit with drivers but would have remained in the dustbin of good ideas if Gentex engineers had not found ways to overcome daunting manufacturing problems. These wide-angle mirrors had to be made by precisely combining a curved area of glass with a constant radius (similar to the convex mirror common on U.S. automobiles) with an outer edge aspheric part that has a gradually increasing curvature. The high curvature in the aspheric area is responsible for the greatly expanded field of view. Bringing these two pieces of glass together with flawless precision challenged

Gentex's excellent team of engineers and required several rounds of process innovation.

Gentex follows a strategy of technology deployment to keep its manufacturing processes at world-class levels, acquiring or developing new approaches. One of the best examples of a company that has simultaneously innovated in product and process technologies, however, is found in Oakville, Ontario: Stackpole, Limited.

➤ Stackpole, Limited's Powdered Metal Parts

Most of us are familiar with the machining of parts and gears from metal blanks or other cast forms. This approach is an important characteristic of the industrial age. Canada's Stackpole, Ltd., has created an alternative to the metal machining process in its development of high load-bearing parts made from powdered metal. This method makes it possible to produce parts with more complex shapes than can be economically machined from conventional forgings, and at substantial cost savings. For example, herringbone gears and offset gears that provide greater power-transfer efficiency and less noise can be produced economically through powdered metal technology. The same designs cannot easily be produced through traditional metal cutting.

The Stackpole sprockets now used in two General Motors' front-wheel-drive transmissions both have been made more durable through Stackpole's innovative SelectDens™ process. One of the transmission sprockets uses a phased-tooth design that cannot be produced through traditional metalworking technologies. This design reduces transmission noise, facilitates greater transmission efficiency, eliminates the need for a steel-bearing sleeve, and costs GM about 30 percent less than a traditional machined sprocket. Borg Warner created this advanced design, but Stackpole's process innovations made manufacturing it feasible.

To trace the development of high load-bearing powdered metal products—and the process that makes them—we must go back more than 50 years. The know-how for molding parts from powdered metal (PM) has been around since World War II, when resource-strapped Germans developed it for using scrapped material. Because the mechanical properties of PM parts were poor, however, they could only be used for low-stress applications.

To make PM parts, the manufacturer pours powdered metal into a mold and compresses it in a die under extreme pressure. After being heated in a sintering furnace—which develops the bonds between the metal particles—and some light machining, the finished part is a good substitute for a steel part in many applications. These die-pressed parts can be made into a wide variety of shapes and at lower costs. If a designer can think of a shape and define it in a mold, the part can be produced. The same cannot be said about steel. Until Stackpole's advancements of this technology, however, these parts did not enjoy a reputation for durability.

Stackpole was one of many companies operating in the PM business during the mid-1980s, cranking out parts for the automobile industry at commodity prices. And like commodity producers in every industry, it was searching for a path to an up-market business. If the company's managers could improve the durability and precision of PM parts, it could command better margins and enter new and larger markets with high-value applications. But the technical problems associated with such a move were daunting.

Enter Peter Jones, a British metallurgist with years of experience and successful innovation in the field of powdered metal forging. Jones, whose philosophy was to break the rules of his specialized trade, aimed to solve his company's technical problems, even though some Stackpole executives thought his chances of success were slim. "Stackpole was only a $15 million company with some forty employees at the time," according to Jones, "so we had this little company with big aspirations." Jones laid out a four-year plan for taking Stackpole into new and more profitable markets, and the senior management team bought into it.

Jones and people brought in to assist him began by dismantling automotive transmissions and identifying parts for which PM alternatives seemed feasible. They also had to identify the properties required for these parts. Both material and process R&D followed. A U.K. company with special skills and machinery was purchased.

After exploratory discussions with General Motors, Jones and his people developed part prototypes using superior alloy compositions. GM had used powdered metal parts in the past, but had been dissatisfied with their performance. After testing Stackpole's prototypes, however, its procurement people liked what they saw. One of these was the first powdered metal clutch plate made for automatic transmissions. GM favored this part over its current powdered metal parts and gave Stackpole a substantial order. Another order soon followed from Chrysler.

Despite these initial successes, Jones's four-year plan fell short of its stated goals and many technical problems remained. The company also needed manufacturing facilities capable of filling its new orders. Undeterred, Jones sought backing for yet another four-year plan that included expansion of the R&D team and an investment of $50 million—an amount roughly equivalent to the company's annual revenue at the time (1993).

Jones's new plan presented Stackpole's management with a difficult choice. They could stick to their traditional business, which had little growth potential, or they could back the promising but highly risky new plan. In the end, they chose the latter. It was, as described by Karl Schein, Stackpole's marketing manager, a "bet the company decision."

The powdered metal challenge involved more than the technology for designing and formulating materials. Process technologies capable of producing these parts in commercial quantities and at high levels of quality had to be developed concurrently. These evolved into five steps, each patented by Stackpole:

1. Special powdered metal formulations.
2. Compacting of these fomulations under pressure in a "split die" shaping device.
3. Hardening of semifinished parts in a vacuum carburizing furnace—the world's largest.
4. High-speed precision grinding.
5. "Selective densification" (SelectDens™), a process for identifying part areas that require strengthening, and putting a thin skin of steel over them.

The first commercialized part to come through the new process was a sprocket designed to replace a traditional steel part for one of General Motors' widely utilized engine transmissions. The next part—another sprocket—took greater advantage of powdered metal's shaping ability; the sprocket's teeth were slightly offset, or phased, with the aim of reducing noise and increasing efficiency. It also reduced the cost to GM by approximately 30 percent.

The combination of product and process innovations made by Stackpole have substantially changed this company and have put it on the road to future growth. Between 1993 and 1998, revenues catapulted from $50 million to $210 million and the number of employees has jumped to about 1,500. Having just scratched the surface of the estimated $50 billion market for auto gears, sprockets, and other high-performance mechanical parts, Stackpole employees are now working vigorously to perfect their new processes and to find new applications. These include an initiative to develop connector rods and a project to develop parts for an entirely new Peugeot-Citroën transmission being designed with the unique shaping capabilities of powdered metal gears in mind. The latter aims to combine three current steel parts into one powdered metal component, resulting in a smaller, quieter, and less costly transmission.

Aside from business performance improvement, Stackpole's exercise in innovation has changed the culture of the company. "People in this division have grown up believing that endless technology challenge and growth is the norm," say Jones. "And so we now have this entrepreneurial company with lots of hard, tough problems to solve."

■ INNOVATIONS IN ORGANIZATIONAL PROCESSES

While innovation in discrete processes is important, we cannot ignore the impact of innovation on broader organizational processes—in particular, the processes for decision making and strategy development. Jim and David Matheson have astutely observed that the past two decades of quality and process improvements have generally stopped short of the executive suite, leaving companies operationally strong but strategically weak:

> *Unlike the ancient Athenians, who recognized the need to develop the body and the mind, efforts to develop and improve the modern organization have concentrated on the body while ignoring the mind that directs it. The frequent result is misdirected effort and wasted accomplishment.*[1]

Process improvement and innovation at the top has tremendous leverage. We all understand the bottom line impact of 10 to 20 percent operational process improvements. But just imagine what would happen, as the Mathesons point out, if top-level decisions and strategies improved to the same extent. Profitability and market share would take quantum leaps forward.

There are many good processes for decision making and problem solving, and you have probably been exposed to several. Most, however, drag out over months, if not years. Few important business problems can wait that long, and stretching out the process over a long period has lots of negative effects: enthusiasm is lost; people become cynical; the situation you're trying to deal with changes; and the day-to-day work of the organization is disrupted.

To overcome this problem, our colleagues at Ernst & Young have developed an innovative process for improving decision making and strategy development—an Accelerated Solutions Environment™, or ASE. As the name implies, an ASE brings people together in a physical space (Figure 5.2) designed to rapidly produce decisions and action plans that would normally take organizations 6 or more months. The collaborative ASE process draws out the best ideas of large groups and, with the help of a staff of professional facilitators, combines those ideas with objective facts and best practices to generate and test concrete decisions and action plans.

The idea of accelerated solutions was first conceived by Matt and Gail Taylor, who refined and applied it to government, the military, nonprofits, and middle-size companies over a period of 20 years. As implemented today by Ernst & Young, it brings together everyone and everything needed to break down a problem and build a solution. It supplements these with technology, information, and skilled facilitators, most of whom operate behind the scene. Everyone works intensely for three days in a specially built facility designed to promote collaborative effort.

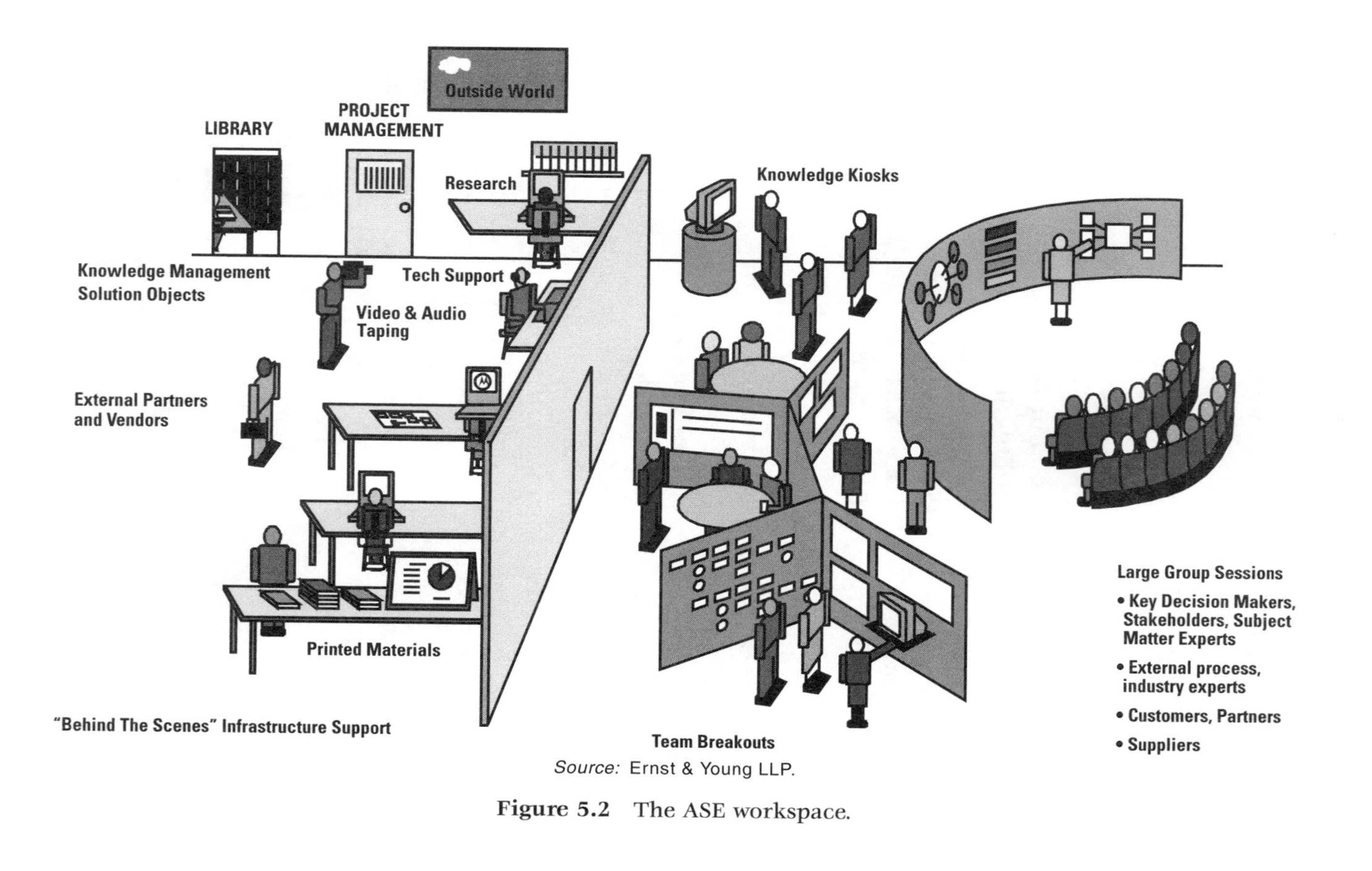

Source: Ernst & Young LLP.

Figure 5.2 The ASE workspace.

Each day represents a different phase of the ASE, and a different set of activities:

- ➤ *Day One—The Scan Phase.* The scan phase forces people to think and work outside their accustomed environments—"outside the box." Facilitator staff people expose participants to industry trends, industry experts, and leading practices. The goals are to develop a common language, uncover critical assumptions, and discover different ways of looking at problems.
- ➤ *Day Two—Focus.* After a day of scanning, participants are prepared to focus on defining the problem at hand. Thanks to scanning, many find that they can now see the problem with new eyes. The bulk of day two is devoted to examining assumptions, evaluating alternative solutions, and confronting barriers to change.
- ➤ *Day Three—Act.* As Ernst & Young ASE director Rob Evans told us, "By the third day people can feel things coming together. They can smell a concrete solution." For the better part of day three, small groups of participants take the strategic view that has converged from the previous two days, and break it into concrete decisions, work plans, time lines, goals, and metrics. The small groups then report back these back to an assembly of all participants for advice and acceptance, creating alignment between units, buy-in, and ownership.

This accelerated process is not for everyone. Our E&Y colleague, Chris Gopal, has observed, "Some companies have cultures that are not aggressive or transformation minded. Those types of companies are not right for this process." But for those with the right stuff, the ASE really works. Our experience with dozens of companies, including American Airlines, Boeing, Carlson Companies, Genentech, Kellogg, Wal-Mart,

DaimlerChrysler, Ford Motor Company, Peugeot-Citroen SA, TRW, and American Axle indicates that participants leave the workshop with more than a big binder and a pile of notes. Instead, they return to their companies with agreement on an overall solution and concrete action steps.

■ THE PROCESS IS THE THING

Many companies continue to focus their attention on managing people instead of processes. Deming was the first to teach us that this focus leads to marginal results at best. Good employees might improve their productivity by 5 percent to 10 percent thanks to managerial attention, and mediocre employees might improve by 10 percent to 20 percent. That's nice but falls far short of the breakthrough improvements made possible through process innovation and continuous process improvement.

People issues—and they are important—can easily distract executives and managers. But they will often create greater success by giving equal attention to the processes through which their companies create value:

- How people are hired and their capabilities developed.
- The interfaces between your company, its customers, and supplier.
- Key processes for developing and manufacturing products.
- Organizational approaches to developing strategy, solving problems, and making major decisions.

Technology

We want to be a leader of any paradigm shift, not a casualty of it.

Chuck Jones
Dana Corporation

One of the great benefits of being a management consultant is the opportunity it affords to witness technological innovation in the making and in its application. Some of the things we see are absolutely amazing—all the more so when they occur in an industry once written off by business pundits as comatose in North America. The Comfort Engineering Laboratory developed by Johnson Controls provides just one example of an innovation that leads to a more successful business and better value for customers.

Customer satisfaction is a complex issue in any industry. In the auto business, it has many dimensions: reliability, safety, operational characteristics (handling, braking, driver visibility, etc.), cost of operating, and passenger comfort. Because auto seating and interiors are its primary businesses, Johnson Controls, Inc. (JCI) knew that it had to go beyond hunches to a more scientific understanding about what constituted satisfaction with its part of the automobile. That's why it created a state-of-the-art "comfort lab"—a center for scientifically measuring the factors that result in passenger comfort. Located in Plymouth, Michigan, the comfort lab is staffed by seven engineers and four technicians. It became operational in 1998 and has proven to be an invaluable resource for generating and testing ideas, demonstrating design trade-offs, and bonding with customers.

The goal of the Comfort Engineering Laboratory is to engineer comfort in seating and the arrangement of interior modules. Its most sophisticated piece of equipment is its virtual reality driving simulator, which features:

- A hydraulic shaker table capable of replicating on-the-road motions and vibrations.
- A cabin in which seating and instruments can be reconfigured for any of the popular vehicle types: small cars, midsize cars, and sport utility vehicles. The full range of driving sensations can be felt within this cabin.
- A computer control system capable of integrating visual, audio, and motion effects.

The Comfort Lab simulator is so sophisticated that it can faithfully replicate the conditions of any road anywhere. Human subjects ride in the simulator—sometimes for hours—while engineers perform a battery of tests aimed a quantifying short- and long-term comfort and the ergonomic characteristics of interior features such as controls and cup holders. A special computer-linked sensor pad conducts "pressure mapping" over time and changing road conditions. Pressure mapping indicates precisely where and to what degree a passenger's back, buttocks, and legs must be supported to prevent discomfort. Information developed through this battery of simulation saves time and money in the designing of vehicle interiors.

Still other computers and specialized software are used as tools to produce more comfortable seating. "We use a family of three-dimensional biomechanical design models developed in conjunction with Michigan State University's biomechanical research lab," says manager Kuntal Thakurta, "to simulate human body position and movements within seating systems." These models replicate human factors of key importance to seat designers: torso articulation, spine curvature, hip angle, leg angles, and so forth. Other CAD software makes it possible for the JCI team to simulate the interactions between a range of passenger shapes and sizes and interior ergonomics.

But drivers and passengers do not stay seated. They get in, get out, and change their sitting positions over the course of any given driving trip. To optimize the seats and interior spaces, these movements must be understood. To gather this information, the Comfort Lab developed a motion analysis system capable of tracking and measuring passenger movements. That information is used designing interior space.

The product of the Comfort Lab's technology is data about how vehicle passengers interact with seating and interiors, and that data gives JCI a competitive advantage in securing contracts with auto OEMs. This data is highly valued by JCI customers. Mike Suman elaborates on this advantage:

> *When we can go to [an OEM] with data from its customer—the consumer—about an idea we've been developing and sit down with [that OEM] in a partnership way and apply that idea in a way that fits the OEM's market niche, we create a win-win situation.*

Technical innovations like the Comfort Lab—whether home-grown or imported from other industries—enable firms to differentiate themselves and their products, thereby gaining competitive advantage. Here are just a few other recent examples of technological innovation that have led to differentiation and competitive advantage. Each qualified as a 1999 PACE Award winner:

➤ *The Goodyear Run-Flat Tire.* Introduced at the 1998 New York Auto Show, Goodyear's Eagle EMT (extended mobility technology) tire allows a car to continue driving at highway speed and without loss of control even when the tire has lost *all* tire pressure. EMT eliminates the danger of changing a flat tire along the shoulder of busy roadways, and it eliminates the need for a spare tire, car jack, tools and the space needed to store them.

The technology, in principle, is simple. The supporting Goodyear technology is a specially formulated and controlled rubber reinforced side wall strengthened to permit an unchanged tire profile without air inflation. Depending on applications and desired driving characteristics, the side wall content can be varied, allowing a range of performance levels. With increasing interest in safety, convenience, cargo space, weight and energy savings, Goodyear is committed to extending application of its new technology to many new models and to the tire aftermarket.

➤ *ASHA's Hydro-Mechanical Coupling Device.* Tiny ASHA Corporation made a major technical breakthrough when it developed and introduced GERODISC™, a coupling device that sends torque to the wheel or wheels that have the most traction, thereby eliminating wheel slippage, and enhancing safety and driver control.

Like most great innovations, the technology is a very simple solution to a very complex problem: in this case, the problem of automotive tractive capacity. It functions invisibly to the driver and provides major improvements in both handling and traction. It also replaces more expensive, complex, and heavier systems, saving OEMs an estimated $75 and 55 pounds per vehicle, with even larger potential savings due to the elimination of current front wheel drive architecture. No wonder OEMs love doing business with innovative suppliers!

➤ *The Motorola MPC555 PowerPC microcontroller with embedded flash memory.* Automobiles and trucks have used microcontrollers for a number of years. Prior to the introduction of Motorola's game-changing innovation, however, different functions and different vehicles required different controllers, creating complexity in manufacturing, inventory, installation, and servicing. Some vehicles would have five different computers, each located in a different area and assigned the job of controlling different functions: fuel injection; air bag deployment; steering controls; yaw sensors in the suspension; and so on. Nothing tied them together. Further, because these controllers were highly sensitive to vibrations and temperature variations, they could not be located in or near the engine, but had to be crammed into dashboard space.

The MPC555 micro controller changed the rules of the game. It created a central command center capable of replacing many separate and uncoordinated control functions. Packaging and complexity are reduced. And because of its flash memory, "one size fits all"—it can support engine types from four to twelve cylinders using all types of fuels, including hybrids, and can handle all power train operations. Software unique to each engine

THE PAYOFF OF GOOD R&D

Our 1999 PACE finalists reported a growing rate of return from new technologies. Those implemented in 1993 returned an average 13 percent. New technologies implemented in 1997, however, have averaged a return of more than 29 percent. With such high rewards for implementing technology-based solutions and system, it is no wonder that 80 percent of technology-oriented projects are implemented by these same companies.

type can be installed before or *after* the controller is mounted, making adjustments possible at any time prior to or after vehicle assembly. In addition, the MPC555 can be mounted in the hostile environment of the engine compartment or inside the transmission, preserving higher value real estate in the passenger cabin.

■ BRIDGING DISCONTINUITIES

Some innovations are so fundamental that they shake the very foundations of an industry, fitting Joseph Schumpeter's definition of innovation as a force for creative destruction. "Whenever technological discontinuities occur," wrote Richard Foster, "companies' fortunes change dramatically."[1] We need only look to history to appreciate Foster's remark and the extent to which powerful, well-financed, and ably managed industry leaders can be toppled by upstarts when one era of technology gives way to another. AT&T once controlled all long-distance phone service and phone equipment manufacturing in the United States. Since the early 1980s, however, deregulation and new technology have created a new cellular phone industry dominated by Motorola and a handful of others, all new players in the telecommunications game. Digital computing provides another example. Not long ago that industry was dominated by less than a handful of mainframe makers, IBM being far and away the most prominent. Today, technical innovation has made computing power faster, cheaper, and highly distributable. A wave of upstarts—Microsoft, Intel, Compaq, Dell—have captured this new industry.

The way in which an established technology is displaced by another—and the consequences—has been nicely explained by MIT's James Utterback through the

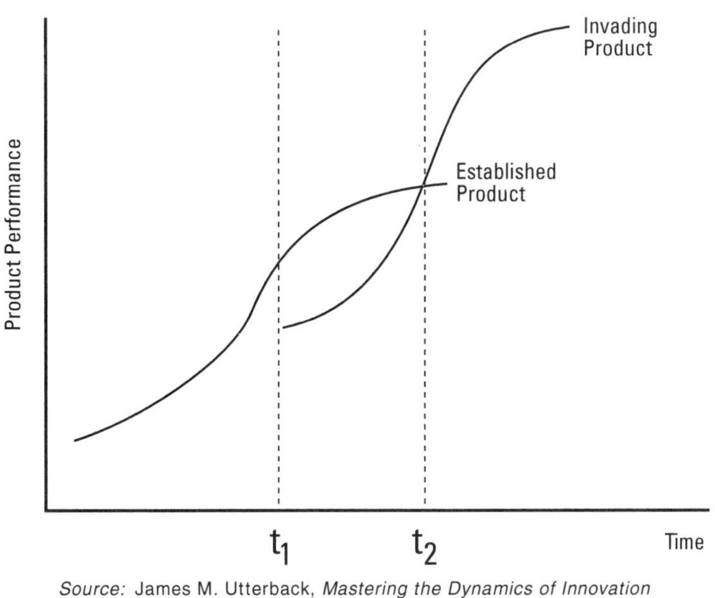

Source: James M. Utterback, *Mastering the Dynamics of Innovation* (Boston, MA: Harvard Business School Press, 1994), 158–59.

Figure 6.1 Performance of an established and an invading product contrasted.

traditional S-curve. As shown in Figure 6.1, technologies typically go through a period of rapid improvement in performance (or cost reduction) followed by another period in which the pace of performance improvements tapers off. If an invading technology enters the picture late in the life cycle of an old technology, it stands a good chance of matching and then leaping ahead of the old technology, rendering it obsolete:

> *At the time an invading technology first appears (t_1), the established technology generally offers better performance or cost than does the challenger, which is still unperfected. . . . The new technology may be viewed objectively as crude, leading to the belief that it will find only limited application. The performance superiority of the established technology may*

> *prevail for quite some time. . . . Eventually, the newcomer improves its performance characteristics to the point where they match those of the established technology (t_2) and rockets past it, still in the midst of a period of rapid improvement.*[2]

Utterback's research provides many examples of how companies have managed to improve the performance of the established technology through aggressive incremental improvements (e.g., turboprop technology did this for piston-driven aircraft engines). But this simply forestalls the inevitable. At some point, established companies must either acquire the skills they need to make the leap to the new technology, or compete from a position of technical weakness. This is exactly the situation faced by Delphi Saginaw Steering in the early 1990s as electronics stood poised to invade its traditional business. To paraphrase a report we issued several years ago, "Truly innovative companies are always going out of the businesses they are in, and, through innovation, entering new ones."[3]

Making the leap to the next wave (or S-curve) of technology is extremely difficult. Harvard professor Clay Christensen has taken Utterback's analysis a step further in explaining why well-financed and "well-managed corporations that have their competitive antennae up, listen astutely to their customers, [and] invest aggressively in new technologies"[4] still lose market dominance when disruptive technologies enter the scene. In his view, the virtues that sustain these companies in their day-to-day business—customer focus and allocation of resources to the most profitable product lines—ultimately weaken them. In many respects, companies are held captive by their current customers and their short-term needs. As Christensen described the "innovation dilemma" in an interview:

> *Many high-performing companies have well-developed systems for killing ideas and products that their customers don't*

> *want. It's part of an entrenched philosophy that focuses resources on the most lucrative markets of the moment. As a result, these companies find it very difficult to invest in disruptive technologies—low margin opportunities that their customers don't want at that time—until their customers realize they want them. And by then, it's too late.*
>
> *Companies that demand market data and financial justification before pursuing a new possibility are vulnerable—in fact, their hesitation actually helps faster, more entrepreneurial companies to catch the next great wave of industry growth, making it progressively more difficult for them to enter the even newer small markets destined to become the larger ones of the future. Finding new applications and markets for new products seems to be a capability that many successful firms exhibited once, only to surrender it as they establish a strong customer base and fall victim to the "good company" practices that brought down their predecessors.*[5]

Indeed, many of the business practices that managers have been taught to follow make the challenge of catching the next wave of technology more difficult, especially if they work for big corporations. Here are two practices that appear to *inhibit* technical progress when followed too enthusiastically:

1. *Listening too closely to customers (and the customer's customer).* With some exceptions, customers are not the source of innovative ideas, if only because they know little or nothing about the technical possibilities. Chrysler's Robert Lutz made this point when he said that no customer ever asked for the cab-forward design introduced by his company. Instead of giving you good ideas, most customers will tell you to continue what you're already doing: "Give us a cheaper or better version of your current product." If you are their information technology supplier, for example, customers will *not* tell you to create a new computer

system that will render their current system and its custom-tailored software obsolete. Instead, they'll want you to upgrade what they already own. Both IBM's mainframe business and the late Digital Equipment Corporation appear to have been victims of this "tyranny of the served market."

2. *Focusing myopically on big markets.* Financial hurdles at big companies are generally so high that technologists and product developers are forced *by policy* to aim for big markets with existing customers. This constraint explains why true innovations are so often brought to market by small entrepreneurial firms,

THE *RIGHT* CUSTOMERS

While most experts warn us to avoid listening *too* closely to customers, Vincent Barabba suggests that companies listen to the "right" customers. In his definition, the right customers include:

➤ Innovators—the people who are always the first on their block to acquire a new product concept.

➤ Opinion leaders—those who informally influence the thinking and behavior of others in particular product categories.

➤ Lead users—pioneering adopters of new products who buy off-the-shelf products and adapt them in ways that their producers never conceived. MIT's Eric von Hippel has demonstrated the utility of lead users in *Sources of Innovation* (New York: Oxford University Press, 1988).

Source: Vincent P. Barabba, *Meeting of the Minds* (Boston, MA: Harvard Business School Press, 1995, 134–35.

> which can operate profitably in small markets. And, as often happens, the new technologies that tap these small markets make performance gains over time, find more and broader applications, and eventually *create* huge unanticipated new markets. By that time, the big companies are so far behind on the learning curve that they have no chance of getting on board.

There are no easy solutions to the innovation dilemma that Christensen has identified. However, if a company does three things well, it is more likely to bridge technical discontinuities as they appear: (1) scan for technologies that represent threats or opportunities, (2) adhere to a *process* for systematically identifying and developing tomorrow's core capabilities, and (3) find ways to intelligently import and apply technologies developed in other industries to your own business.

■ SCANNING

Every technology-based company must regularly ask itself two questions:

1. What is going on out there that could kill our business?
2. What is going on out there that we could use to assure industry leadership?

Most innovative companies seek the answers to these questions through scanning mechanisms. In the early 1970s, James R. Bright advocated systematic monitoring of the external environment, and that advice remains potent to this day.[6] His advice was to:

- ➤ Look for the forerunners of significant technological change.
- ➤ When you find them, identify the consequences.
- ➤ Measure the developmental speed of the emerging technology and verify its direction.
- ➤ Report findings to senior management.

The Internet can be an exceptional scanning tool. However, to make the most of it, scanners must first define their information needs and create structures for capturing and distributing information.

Dana Corporation has a staff person assigned to the job of doing key-word searches of databases for its R&D personnel. This is one of the ways that Dana scans for new technical developments. Every day, these personnel receive printed output from these searches. Most of it is useless information that ends up in the recycling bin, but every so often a searcher identifies something of real value.

Scanning is obviously important, but where should a company scan? Most organizations make the mistake of limiting scanning operations to their immediate industry and circle of competitors. This is what the financial services companies did all through the 1980s and 1990s as they tried to identify different strategies for capturing the assets of savers and investors. What were the banks doing? What were the big brokerage houses and insurance companies doing? And what about the mutual fund companies?

In the end, the big financial services firms were blindsided by technologies and changes taking place outside their scanning circle. They were so buy watching each other that they failed to see how the Internet would spawn a new option for personal money management: online trading; and easily accessible advice and company research. These new options have made the service of traditional providers less and less valuable to active customers.

The most disruptive technological innovations are very often introduced by newcomers and industry outsiders—people whom no one bothers to monitor. The fuel cell technology described later in this chapter was developed by nonplayers in the automotive market, but it may very well create the most sweeping change that industry has experienced since Ford implemented the assembly line. Likewise, digital imaging, which will surely wipe out film photography in our lifetime, wasn't introduced by Kodak or Fuji, but by Sony, an electronics company.

■ TECHNOLOGICAL INNOVATION AS PROCESS

Moving a company from one generation of technology to the next is a major challenge, particularly when existing customers and the bulk of current earnings are locked into an older technology. Perhaps the surest way to manage this difficult transition is through a deliberate and explicit process that identifies and builds the technical competencies the organization will need in the future. Motorola developed such a process during the 1970s under the Technology Roadmap Program. This program, which was institutionalized within each technical unit, aimed to sketch out the current technologies of interest to the company, potential new ones, market needs, and competitive comparisons. These were considered within time frames. The program had four important features:[7]

1. Dual commitment by both divisional management and the CEO to everything on the roadmap.

2. Semiannual reviews.
3. Documentation and data tracking.
4. Minority reports for each roadmap review to assure that projects that failed to gain support would have a second hearing.

That program has obviously helped Motorola move forward in the rapidly changing field of electronics. In the industry we know best, automotive, we have found another useful process for engaging the confusing business of new technology, this one developed by Dana Corporation.

Dana is the world's largest independent supplier of vehicle components, modules, and systems. It makes axles, frames, and engine components. That may sound like a stodgy business, but to remain competitive, its scientific and engineering personnel must stay on top of technical developments in metallurgy, metal shaping and cutting, and electronics. To accomplish this within a highly decentralized organization, Dana has developed a bottom-up technology process through which future technical requirements are identified by individual units and then pursued through a cross-divisional team effort. Figure 6.2 provides a rough outline of this process.

The reason for making the process cross-divisional is that Dana's operating units share many, if not most, of its technological capabilities. According to Technology VP Chuck Jones, "Technology is applicable across division lines and is applicable to more than one component. Electronics is a big part of our future in terms of 'smart' systems, closed-loop control systems." Brakes, suspensions, engine components, and hydraulic systems are all highly integrated with electronics. Thus, Dana has to address the applications of microprocessors and electronics across division lines.

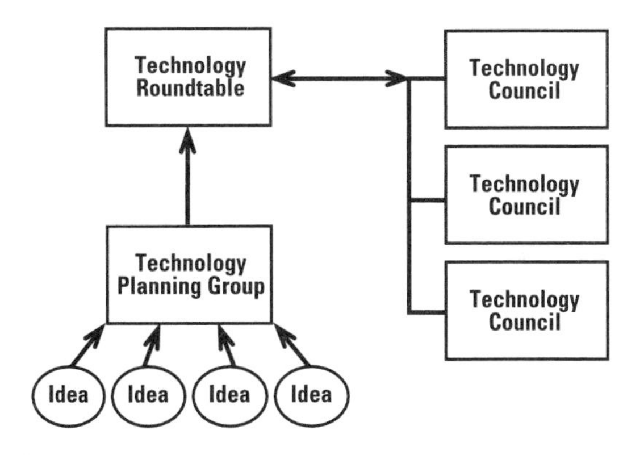

Figure 6.2 Dana's technology process.

The goal of the company's technology process is to identify and pursue a manageable number of "emerging core technologies" (ECTs) that are:

- Either nonexistent or underutilized within the company.
- Deemed vital to Dana's future.

Here's how the process works. Personnel in each operating division submit their ideas about important new technologies to a Technology Planning Group, which screens the ideas, combines them when appropriate, and submits the most compelling to the semiannual meeting of the corporation's Technology Roundtable. The Roundtable includes the corporation's highest-ranking executives—including the CEO and President—and the divisional directors of engineering. Roundtable members debate the merits of each idea submitted and vote on whether it merits emerging core technology status. Each ECT becomes the focus of a Technology Council, whose sole job is to learn as much as possible about its assigned ECT, track its progress, and begin developing

THE ELECTRONIC VEHICLE COUNCIL

Dana's Electronic Vehicle Council provides a good example of how following a dynamic technology process can help a company identify and bridge technological discontinuities.

Dana's VP of Technology Planning, Chuck Jones, has followed developments in electric vehicles (EVs) for more than a decade, and notes that until very recently *none* of the mainline automakers or auto suppliers had a presence in the promising new field of fuel cell vehicles. Even as late as 1999, conferences on fuel cell technology were dominated by companies that most people never heard of—companies like Ballard and Plug Power, a joint venture of DTE Energy Company (the parent of Detroit Edison) and Mechanical Technology, Inc.

Fuel cell technology, if successful, would dramatically change the automotive economy. A fuel cell converts the energy of a fuel (hydrogen, natural gas, methanol, gasoline, etc.) and air or oxygen into direct current electricity, and with only the most benign environmental consequences. Unlike traditional fossil fuel power plants, fuel cells generate no carbon monoxide, nitrogen, or sulfur oxide emissions. Furthermore, a significant percentage of the heat produced by fuel cells can be captured and reused, eliminating significant releases of thermal pollution. Fuel cells also possess important advantages over the battery power technology that has sustained EV development in the past. First, there is no downtime for recharging. Second, and more important, a fuel cell vehicle would not be limited in its operating duration or achievable top speed; unlike a battery-powered EV, it would theoretically operate at a wide range of speeds and for as long as fuel was supplied.

A major breakthrough in fuel cell technology would have monumental implications for many companies. Today's internal combustion engines would be replaced entirely by

(Continued)

smaller, lighter electric motors; heavy and expensive drive trains, axles, engine cradles, mufflers, exhaust manifold, catalytic converters, and other supporting elements of traditional engines would no longer be needed. Power Plug and Ford Motor Company have already entered into a joint effort to commercialize this technology, and DaimlerChrysler, GM, and Toyota are pursuing similar programs.

Electric utilities and heating companies would likewise be faced with major challenges if small, affordable fuel cells units were to become available to residential and commercial customers—something toward which General Electric and Plug Power are already jointly working.

Dana's ability to work with it. An ECT is not tied to any Dana product or division. There are currently 10 Technology Councils at Dana. Process participants learned years ago that a larger number would spread the company's resources too thin.

Membership in Dana's Technology Councils is cross-divisional and is extended to directors of engineering and to employees with particular expertise in the assigned emerging core technology. In addition, representatives of other companies are periodically brought in to share their knowledge.

In keeping with the Dana Style of internal self-sufficiency, every effort is made to develop ECT capabilities internally. In some cases, however, the company acquires outside expertise. Chuck Jones related this story about one Technical Council and how it used the process to develop an ECT of growing importance:

> *For years, we produced frames and axles, but we did not engineer or produce the suspension between them. We didn't even know how to deal with the vehicle dynamics that cuts across*

axles, suspensions, and frames. But over the past two years using the Vehicle Dynamics Suspension Council, we've grown the expertise. We hired a suspension engineer with ten years of experience from Ford Motor Company to head up the effort. After a year and a half of development and training, Dana now has very good competency in suspension design. And it all started with a group of people sitting around a table saying "We're dumb in this area and we have to fix it."

The technology process just described is very well understood throughout the Dana Corporation. When employees develop ideas about technology, or when they identify technological threats and opportunities, they know where to go with them. Dana's existing Electronic Vehicle Council, for example, developed through this process. "When we first started this process," says Chuck Jones, "Dana wasn't even looking at electric vehicles or hybrids or fuel cells. Now we're involved with all of them and with fuel cell component development." After almost a dozen years of watching EV technologies, Dana had become a full participant—something that would never have happened had it simply stuck to its knitting in the fields of axles, frames, and drive trains.

At the same time, employees have the assurance that their ideas will be considered through a rational process of screening and review reaching to the very top echelons of the company. An important side benefit of the process, according to Jones is that senior managers are always kept current with the latest technical developments coming down the pike.

■ TECHNOFUSION

Innovative companies acquire and adapt technologies both from within and outside their divisions or industries. For example, both TRW and Delphi used software expertise from their respective aerospace and defense divisions to assist in the development of their electronic steering and suspension products. Having software development, program management, and systems integration capabilities was critical to the success of the eventual products. Rather than develop or build them internally, both companies took the faster approach of assimilating these skills from sister divisions.

Many innovations result from the integration of multiple technical capabilities, such as mechanical, optical, and electrical systems with computer software. The result is team-based innovation beyond the grasp of a single "inventor." The Auto-Clear Rain Sensor developed by Control Devices provides a fitting example. It combined traditional mechanical engineering expertise with software engineering from their aerospace and defense division in designing electrical steering systems. Likewise, JCI and Bosch (both PACE winners) combined innovation in postconsumer recyclable materials with their existing product engineering expertise to produce new product concepts.

The idea of "technofusion" is not new. In his tales of innovations past and present, James Utterback has explained how the first typewriter borrowed from earlier inventions.

> *The Scholes typewriter was a synthesis of a number of existing mechanical technologies. . . . The telegraph machine and piano provided models for the keys, and mechanical clock gears suggested a means of shifting from line to line. . . . Joined together, they created something new. The early electrics likewise joined together familiar components (small electric motors and manual typewriters) to create a new machine. Even the very radical leap to personal computer technology carried with it the old and the familiar: The QWERTY keyboard, typing conventions, and so forth. . . . The personal computer itself was built from available components created by other sectors of the electronics industry: television monitors,*

printed circuit boards, memory chips, semiconductors, and the like.[8]

PACE winners acquire and adapt technologies both from within and from outside their own industries. Examples range from advanced computer software used in moviemaking and aerospace technologies to advanced electronics and recycling practices. The PACE judges see a growing fusion of technologies being exploited among fast-track innovators. Many innovations result from the integration of high-level capabilities, such as mechanical, optical, electrical, material, and software. The Auto-Clear™ Rain Sensor developed by Control Devices, Inc. required that company to integrate electronics, software, and optics—plus a purchasing base for European distribution.

Control Devices' patented device enhances existing intermittent wiper systems to improve vehicle occupant comfort and safety. Auto-Clear imitates the human eye while analyzing moisture and the rate of its accumulation on the windshield. The sensor immediately determines the appropriate wiper speed and automatically activates the wiper system. Auto-Clear accommodates varying rain conditions by adjusting wiper speed; its noncontact design senses fog or moisture on the interior glass and controls the vehicle's defogger system. This unit's attachment to the rear-view mirror allows for easy installation on the production line and easy remount if the windshield is replaced.

■ GETTING A HANDLE ON TECHNOLOGICAL CHANGE

The quotation at the beginning of this chapter captures the perils and promise of technological change. Ignore it and your business will soon be eclipsed. Engage with it and you have a fighting chance of living to fight again.

The surest way to get a handle on technological change is to create a process that allows you to scan the road ahead and review your own strategy for travel on that road. Current and incubating technologies have time-paced trajectories. Someone should have responsibility for mapping those trajectories and communicating them to decision makers and technical personnel.

Remember to scan outside the fences of your own industry. More often than not, the best opportunities for technofusion appear in someone else's backyard.

Innovation in the Supply Chain

Today assembly is the easy part. The hard part is managing your suppliers and the flow of parts.

Victor Fung

Not so long ago, most of us viewed market competition in terms of one entity pitted against others. General Motors versus Ford, Chrysler, and a host of offshore automakers. Compaq versus Dell, Hewlett-Packard, Packard-Bell, and Acer. Boeing versus AirBus. AT&T versus MCI and Sprint. This notion of competition is giving way to a broader view in which one *supply chain* is pitted against others. Thus, it is no longer Ford against its traditional rivals, but the entire supply chain of Ford Motor Company, its component suppliers and dealers, against those of its rivals. This is particularly true as companies focus more closely on core activities and outsource the rest—a trend in many industries. How well Ford manages its relationships with suppliers and distributors, as well as its own internal operations, and creates an efficient flow of information and products to customers, plays a substantial role in its success or failure.

Value Web™ is the new and more appropriate name for supply chain since the process of design and production is no longer linear but collaborative. Organizational elements of manufacturers and multiple suppliers work simultaneously on the design of modules, components, location of product logistics, and many other factors. Supply web also reflects the growing use of the web in the sharing of information and executive transactions.

Supply-web-wide solutions are increasingly viewed as the only way to achieve meaningful and lasting cost reductions and improvements in customer service. And there's plenty of room for innovation in these solutions. Li & Fung, Hong Kong's largest export trading company, is a master in the art of supply management. Though it owns not a single factory, Li & Fung commands a network of information systems, shippers, financiers, and 7,500 suppliers scattered across 26 countries that—under its coordination—can deliver high-quality finished goods (primarily consumer goods) to European and North American retails in a matter of weeks of receiving an order. Here's how Victor Fung, the company's chairman describes its operations:

> *Say we get an order from a European retailer to produce 10,000 garments. It's not a simple matter of our Korean office sourcing Korean products or our Indonesian office sourcing Indonesian products. For this customer we might decide to buy yarn from a Korean producer but have it woven and dyed in Taiwan. So we pick the yarn and ship it to Taiwan. The Japanese have the best zippers and buttons, but they manufacture them mostly in China. Okay, so we go to YKK, a big Japanese zipper manufacturer, and we order the right zippers from their Chinese plants. Then we determine that, because of quotas and labor conditions, the best place to make the garments is Thailand. So we ship everything there. And because the customer needs quick delivery, we may divide the order across five factories in Thailand. Effectively,*

we are customizing the value chain to best meet the customer's need.

Five weeks after we have received the order, 10,000 garments arrive on the shelves in Europe, all looking like they came from one factory, with colors, for example, perfectly matched. Just think about the logistics and coordination. This is a new type of value added, a truly global product that has never been seen before.[1]

What Fung and other masters of supply management are doing is revolutionary. They are dissecting the entire Value Web of manufacturing and shipping and seeking the best solution for every step, often on a global basis, with the goal of stripping away cost and time.

■ WHAT IS SUPPLY MANAGEMENT?

Value Web management is the coordinated flow of materials, information, and products across the enterprise and with trading partners.[2] In traditional supply management, the flow of materials and products moves from one entity to another and in a series of discrete, arm's-length transactions. Collaboration on customer issues, product design, and information sharing is minimal. OEMs pit one supplier against another to hold down costs and to prevent any one supplier from acquiring economic leverage. One of the most notable cases of this tradition involved Jose Ignacio Lope de Arriortua, then of General Motors, whose success in creating competition between suppliers and in renegotiating supplier contracts is estimated to have saved GM some $3 to $4 billion.

This traditional model of supply management remains the norm for many companies today. A number of excellent companies, however—Becton Dickinson, Boeing, 3M, Hewlett

Packard, Black & Decker, and many auto producers among them—have discarded the traditional model in favor of a new one that invites suppliers to participate as design partners, risk sharers, and insurers of customer satisfaction. The following list summarizes the characteristic differences between these two models of supply management:

The Old	*The New*
Many suppliers.	Few suppliers.
Arm's-length relationships; playing one partner off against another.	Partner relationships.
Price-based supplier evaluation.	Supplier evaluation based on collaboration and ability to add value.
Make to OEM's specifications.	Collaboration on design.
Centralized purchasing.	Concurrent procurement.
Separate information systems.	Information integration with suppliers.
Suppliers are interchangeable.	Supplier relationships are nurtured.

■ TOWARD COLLABORATION

Collaboration is one of the most important features of new and effective supply webs. It embodies a new paradigm for the interactions that bind buyer and seller, assembler and supplier, even among functions within a company.

When collaboration is high, one-way information flows become two-way. Networks replace walls that once separated different groups. Assets are moved quickly to where they are needed most, regardless of who owns them. The very concept of *owning* assets is being challenged as companies realize that the output of production is what truly carries value, not the means.

Several progressive stages mark the evolutionary road that the best supply webs have followed. Beginning with the "open market negotiations" that characterizes traditional supply relationships, firms move progressively through stages of cooperation and coordination before real collaboration takes place (Figure 7.1).

The boundaries that contain one set of enterprise activities change in two important ways. First, they become permeable, facilitating the movement of personnel and information between separate enterprises. For example, the bill-of-materials for the Mack truck chassis is no longer maintained by Mack but by a key supplier, Dana Corporation. Likewise, when you order a new PC from Dell Computer Corporation, your monitor is shipped directly to you from Dell's monitor supplier, never passing through the Dell warehouse; this takes time and costs out of product delivery. Information systems make it possible for the two firms to collaborate closely in serving the final customer.

Second, the unofficial boundaries of cooperation and collaboration are progressively expanded to bring all

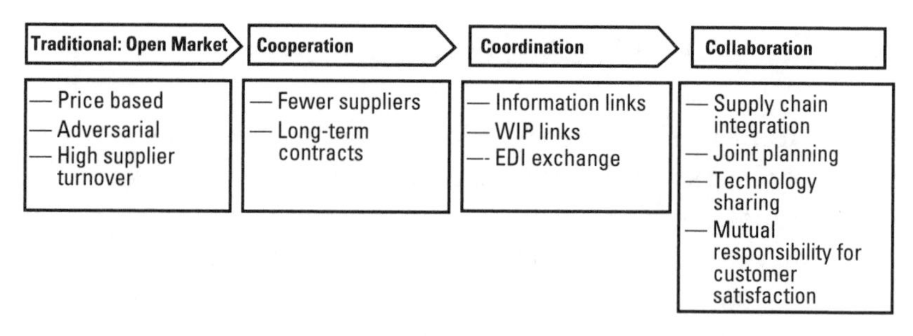

Figure 7.1 The evolutionary path.

value-adding enterprises within a wider boundary that includes the final customer, as shown in Figure 7.2.

In Figure 7.2, the hardened boundaries that initially surround all members of the Value Web—suppliers, OEMs, and customers—eventually become permeable, first between OEM's and the final customer. Suppliers are eventually brought into the party, allowing open exchange of ideas, work, and information.

➤ The Auto Industry Example

In the auto industry, the evolution just described is advancing rapidly. The arm's-length, transactional relationship of the past between OEMs and suppliers is becoming history.

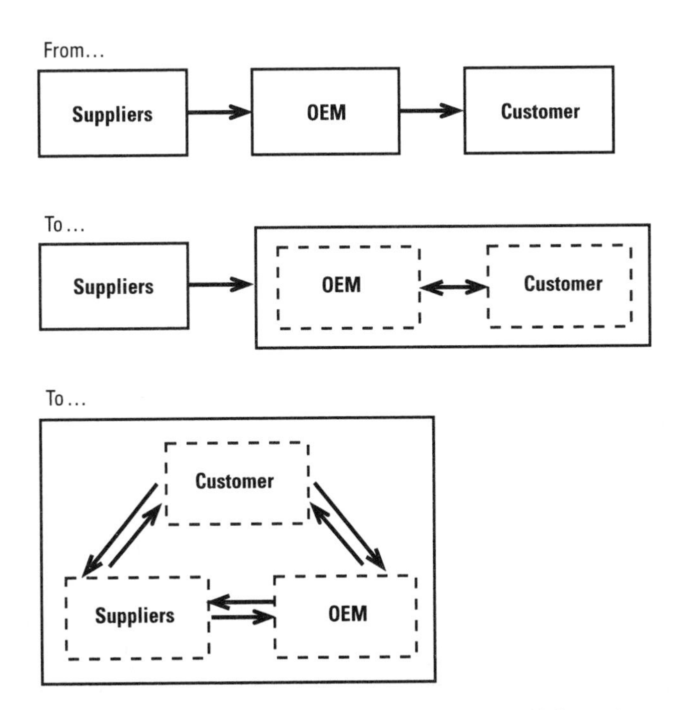

Figure 7.2 Expanding the boundaries of collaboration.

Instead of producing "to print" for commodity prices, auto suppliers are now joining their customers, the OEMs, in planning, engineering, and developing new systems and components. This collaboration generally pays off in better margins, improved components, and long-term contracts for suppliers. Suppliers are even setting up shop inside GM and Chrysler plants. The latter's new transmission plant in Kokomo, Michigan, is now a full-time home for 30 to 40 supplier personnel; these individuals have responsibility for monitoring part quality, meeting with workers on assembly issues, and collaborating with Chrysler engineers, quality teams, and business planning personnel. When problems arise, or when work processes change, the on-site supplier personnel participate in finding new solutions.

Chrysler has gone further than other North American automakers in blurring the boundaries that once separated it and its suppliers. In addition to the preceding example, it has developed a substantial knowledge-sharing arrangement with suppliers that links what it knows about engineering, lessons learned, and best practices, to a unique and secure equivalent database supported by suppliers (more on this in Chapter 8). The objective is to enhance joint decision processes, product/process outcomes, and—ultimately—the business performance of all concerned (Figure 7.3).

What's currently missing from the revolution in auto industry supply management is innovation in the distribution segment of the Value Web, which is little changed from that of previous decades, and which accounts for an estimated 30 percent of vehicle cost at the retail level. In North America, the world's largest automobile market, all producers—including Japanese firms—continue to respond to dealer demand, not final customer demand. Vehicles are produced in *anticipation* of customer orders. The result is that about 95 percent of U.S. vehicles are *dealer-ordered* and purchased off the lot. This creates a disconnect between OEMs and their

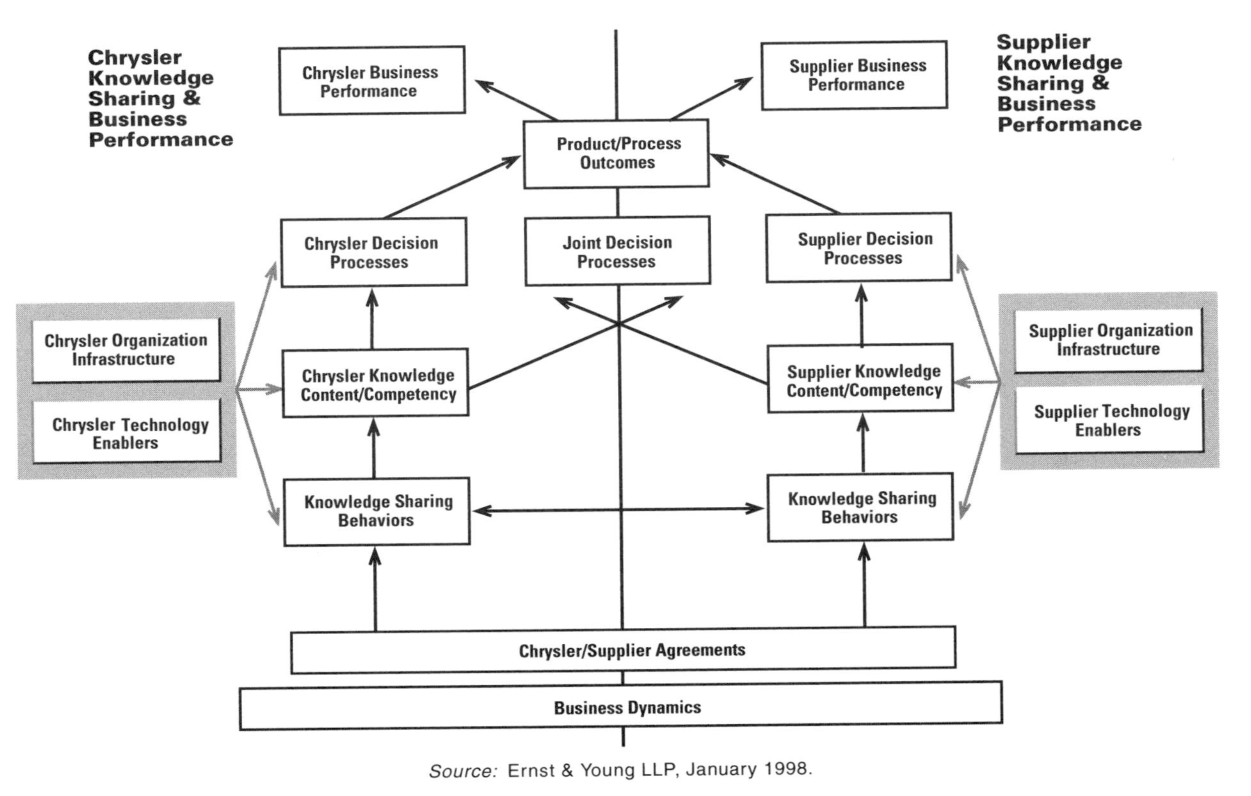

Source: Ernst & Young LLP, January 1998.

Figure 7.3 Knowledge sharing for mutual benefit.

final customers. And since any given model is available in tens of thousand of variations (as to engine size, color, and other option choices), the system practically guarantees that few customers buy the cars they would ideally want.

To support the current system, a typical auto dealer sits on 60 days of inventory. In the absence of reliable forecasting information, dealers maintain inventory. They feel that inventory is the only way to offer a broad array of models and option choices to potential customers. This is an extremely costly approach. The value of that inventory in the United States alone is estimated at approximately $50 billion. This nonproductive investment has negative implications. The most obvious of these is the cost of financing $50 billion in working capital. There is also the problem of "lot rot." Unlike a fine Bordeaux, a mass-produced automobile doesn't get better with age. It is a *wasting* asset. After a car sits for months on a dealer's lot, electrical connections and batteries start to go bad. Even tires may need rebalancing. And many must be marked down as "last year's models." Both working capital and lot rot costs are paid by OEMs, dealers, and customers.

There's a tremendous business case for altering the traditional vehicle distribution system, the most obvious solution being a *pull-through* production system that begins when a customer—not a dealer—places an order. Such a system could reduce order-to-delivery time from 65 days to 15 days and take thousands of dollars out of the cost of the typical motor vehicle.

Although unfinished, the revolution in supply management already marks a welcomed end of an era in which North American auto companies were vertically integrated and did the bulk of their sourcing from captive component suppliers. Insulated from market pressures, few of those captive suppliers developed leading edge performance with the result that their parent companies got the

THE INTERNET AND THE AUTO INDUSTRY: A LOOK AHEAD

Business-to-business and business-to-consumer e-Commerce in general is growing exponentially and is expected to exceed $400 billion by 2002.

To date, e-Commerce in the auto industry has largely been limited to image-building applications and to support for consumer information-gathering. In 1998, a J.D. Power study indicated that 25 percent of all new-vehicle buyers used the Internet to obtain product and pricing information during the shopping process. By 1999, that number had grown; NetSmart reported that of the 53 million people with Internet access in 1999, 61 percent accessed the Net in some way while buying a car—that's 32.3 million people. It is not difficult to visualize the next step: ordering a vehicle from the producer's Web page, with all important options (color, engine size, etc.) chosen directly by the customer. This would drastically alter the currently suboptimized final section of the auto supply web: distribution.

The value of the Net to Value Web partners is even more profound. That effort will be facilitied by the Automotive Network Exchange (ANX) system being developed by an industry consortium. ANX will facilitate communications between OEMs and suppliers in such areas as materials ordering and logistics, increasing the closeness and complexity of supply chain relationships.

worst of all possible worlds: little innovation, high costs, and poor quality.

The expanded outsourcing today is due to an accelerating need for high-level expertise, technology, and relevant processes. Since OEMs can't support all the technical competencies required to produce a world-class vehicle, they look to independent suppliers who must play by three important rules:

Rule One. Have a distinctive competence and build it strategically. Elite suppliers observe this rule; their R&D expenditures as a percentage of sales are now approaching 5 percent, and patents are rising. Great companies, like Gentex, even define what they *won't* do.

Rule Two. Become a strategic partner with your best customers. OEMs depend on partners with unique people talents, processes, and technologies. The same holds for relationships between Tier One and Tier Two suppliers. To observe how these partnerships are cemented, look at where the leading suppliers locate their production engineers. The best locate many of them within OEM facilities. The percentage of these placements rose from 18 percent to almost 60 percent in just four years. Furthermore, joint product development is now common practice among elite suppliers and their customers.

Rule Three. Excel at problem-solving, efficiency, and innovation. The best suppliers are always getting better at developing and applying unique competencies that address customer needs.

■ SUPPLY MANAGEMENT IMPROVEMENTS PAY

The old approach to supply management is well understood by industrial companies and supported by policies, practices, and infrastructure. The question for these companies is: "Why change?" To find out, Ernst & Young and the Darden School of Management engaged in a study of 22 Value Webs involving companies in North America, South America, and Europe across five broad industry groupings (life sciences, oil and gas, consumer products, utilities, and manufacturing). All practiced the new approach previously described. When we asked them why they had changed, the most frequent responses were:

- ➤ Increase end customer satisfaction.
- ➤ Improve profits.
- ➤ Secure reliable source/market for a particular item.
- ➤ Satisfy supplier/customer request.
- ➤ Reduce overall operating costs.
- ➤ Reduce lead time.
- ➤ Reduce price paid for item class.
- ➤ Improve productivity.
- ➤ Increase margins.

Many of these goals have been achieved. Our Ernst & Young colleagues who specialize in supply management note impressive results for companies that practice effective supply chain management:

➤ IBM solved many of its usual problems with waiting times for parts in newly designed products when it involved purchasing agents in its product development process. Procurement engineers now work with product designers to assure that all parts designed for new computers will be available when the new computers go to manufacturing. These same engineers stay in touch with emerging technologies available through key suppliers, and feed this information to their designer colleagues. This personnel integration has helped IBM to cut product development time almost in half.

➤ Motorola has worked hard to coordinate and integrate supply chain activities across company boundaries. To help this along, it reengineered manufacturing processes in 40 of its facilities, resulting in improved quality, a 50 percent cut in cycle times, and overhead savings of almost $1 billion.

- When it developed its now-popular one-time-use camera, Kodak expanded its boundaries into its customers' territory. It followed the usual practice of assigning the development job to a cross-functional team representing R&D, manufacturing, design, and marketing. However, it also looked outward, extending the boundaries of its project to engage retailers and consumers. Today, these cameras account for substantial sales for Kodak.

These pictures of collaboration are, however, far from typical, and what companies *say* they are doing in supply management often belies their actions. The findings of the Ernst & Young/Darden School study suggest that information sharing is less than open; technical information is shared only when necessary. In addition, mixed signals surface about the importance of price in evaluating a partner. Price remains highly important, and there is some evidence that companies view price as the key attribute in decisions. As expected, OEMs appear to be more purchase price conscious than are sellers, and tend to be less willing to share information.[3] OEMs still embrace collaboration less than supplier partners, perhaps because the latter see greater benefits in this closer relationship.

■ THE RIGHT VALUE WEB FOR YOUR BUSINESS

Ernst & Young/Darden research indicates that companies seek Value Web partners that conform to intuitively obvious traits. They want to do business with partners that have these attributes:

- Are trustworthy.
- Understand their business.
- Support their own view of customer business.
- Are committed to the relationship.
- Provide potential synergy.
- Offer economic benefits.

These traits seem obvious in a potential Value Web partner—so obvious, that we must view them merely as starting points in any business relationship. We must look beyond them to something more strategic, and to something tailored to the characteristics of the enterprise's product or service offerings.

Wharton School's Marshall Fisher has given us important insights into the partner selection problem that go beyond the obvious. His view is that different types of products require different types of Value Webs.[4] So-called functional products—retail staples that people buy and use repeatedly, like groceries, fuel, and so on—have fairly predictable demand characteristics. These characteristics have important business consequences for the seller's supply web: product life cycles are fairly long; margins and product variety are low to modest; and lead times are generous. Cost is critical, which means that inventories must be kept razor-thin and supplier efficiencies must be extremely high. The entire supply web, in fact, must emphasize *efficiency*. Because of predictable demand, writes Fisher, "Companies that make such products are thus free to focus almost exclusively on minimizing physical costs—a crucial goal, given the price sensitivity of most functional products." Partners in the Value Web can create and freeze production and delivery schedules well in advance, and concentrate their attention on optimizing cost savings.

Fisher contrasts these functional products with *innovative* products, for which demand is highly *un*predictable:

high-fashion apparel, consumer and office electronics, and so on. For these products, life cycles and lead times are short, margins are high, and the window of market opportunity opens only briefly. As a consequence, supply webs for these innovative products should be assembled and managed more for *speed and flexibility* than for cost efficiency. "The critical decisions to be made about inventory and capacity," according to Fisher, "are not about minimizing costs but about where in the chain to position inventory and available production capacity in order to hedge against uncertain demand. And suppliers should be chosen for their speed and flexibility, not for their low cost."

As a supply manager you must consider the trade-offs between cost efficiency and speed/flexibility. The worst thing you can be as the maker of a functional product is the high-cost producer. Likewise, if your product is trendy women's clothing, the worst thing you can do is to miss the market by a season. This is not to say, however, that one cannot take measures to gain the best of both worlds. For example, a trendy clothing producer must be fast and flexible in meeting demand, but it can still do a great deal to minimize costs

THE COST OF SUPPLY MANAGEMENT

Managing Value Web activities is not without costs. However, good supply management practices can reduce these costs to a large degree. The Supply Chain Council has shown that the best companies incur only about half of the costs incurred by median performers. In the auto industry, for example, best-in-class companies experience total supply-chain management costs equal to 4.3 percent of revenue. The median for the industry is 8.8 percent.

such as operating "demand pull" production to minimize inventory and obsolescence.

■ INNOVATION IN THE VALUE WEB

We usually associate innovation with new products or processes. As earlier chapters have demonstrated, these innovations are often the keys to cost and performance leadership. We are less accustomed to thinking of Value Web innovation as producing the same result, yet the evidence of its power is all around us. Wal-Mart, for example, does not offer distinctly different retail products to its customers. In terms of location and amenities, its stores are no better than those of Sears, Kmart, or most other mass market retailers. Sure, someone greets you at the door, but who cares? Yet, Wal-Mart has consistently outperformed its rivals for over a decade; the reason is its innovations in Value Web management.

It is unlikely that the average PC user could identify any technical or performance difference between a Dell machine and one built by Hewlett-Packard, IBM, or anyone else. Nevertheless, many like Dell's prices and "design-your-own" offer so much that they will order one over the Internet sight unseen. Dell has built a successful enterprise on its innovative approach to linking itself, component and software suppliers, shippers, and the world of customers. That approach creates product uniqueness out of standard components, keeps Dell's inventory requirements to almost nothing, and assures three important values to customers: the machines they want, low prices, and fast delivery.

In both of these cases—Wal-Mart and Dell—industry leadership has been a clear consequence of innovation in the Value Web. We are observing the same in the automotive industry, though the course of innovation has been more evolutionary than revolutionary. Dana Corporation provides a striking example. Under its CEO, Woody Morcott, Dana has moved from being a component supplier to being an *integrator* of larger and larger component systems—taking on a role once assumed by the OEM. The crowning example of its new role can be seen in its ability to deliver a "rolling chassis" to a vehicle assembly plant. The unit it now delivers to DaimlerChrysler's Brazilian plant, for example, represents almost 30 percent of the value in the plant's final Dodge Dakota pickup truck. The unit is a complete system of frame, axles, suspension, drive train, and wheels, and can be rolled directly onto the plant's final assembly line.

By assuming the role of integrator for these major systems, Dana helps its customer achieve its strategic goal of outsourcing more of the auto-building process. At the same time, Dana serves its own strategic desire to move upstream and capture a greater share of industry relationships and to assume responsibility for a broader span of value-adding activities.

Dana's thrust into this larger role is not unique. As PACE Director of Judging William Sharfman has noted:

> *We are seeing an acceleration in both "territory capture" and development of systems integration capabilities around existing central competencies. The leaders seem to find effective ways to innovate and deliver value by broadening as well as deepening the array of related products and services they have on offer. . . . The most effective innovators typically possess and support competencies in understanding customers and customer opportunities, and in ideation, conception, design engineering, invention, prototyping, technology transfer, and applied R&D. Other suppliers display real excellence in execution, in mastery of manufacturing process matters or service management and delivery. But leaders and winners in today's automotive supply chain are seen to do* both *exceedingly well, and usually in a seamless fashion. Those who do*

both, the winners, get the maximum payoff from their innovation by delivering the greatest total value to their customers.[5]

■ YOUR CHALLENGE: GET *CONNECTED*

When most businesspeople and engineers think about innovation, few think about the Value Web as a place where it can make a difference. This chapter has made the value of supply web innovation apparent.

At bottom, innovation in the supply web is about creating and using *connections*. For some companies, these connections are more valuable than balance sheet assets. The case of Li & Fung makes this clear. It does not own a square foot of factory space, but its connections make it a key player in a web of activities that involve almost a million workers in hundreds of plants scatter around Asia. Li & Fung's key assets are its connections and its ability to use them to optimize the activities of suppliers on behalf of customers.

What are your company's connections inside and outside corporate boundaries? How well are you developing and using them to drive out cost and increase speed and variety? Are you pursuing transactions or competing for a share of relationships in your industry? How you answer these questions will say a great deal about the competitiveness of your company.

The need for getting connected goes far beyond setting up a "cool" web site. Much has been said and written about the consumer-direct and Internet-powered business models of Dell, Gateway, and Amazon. Much less has been said about the hard part of e-Commerce: What goes on after a customer clicks the yes box that confirms an order and zaps it through cyberspace to the vendor's Value Web. Fast, accurate fulfillment is what separates the real masters of e-Commerce from wannabes with web pages.

Dell and Gateway have demonstrated the power of being tightly connected with their customers and their supply web partners. Both allow buyers to customize their purchases, and both have mastered fulfillment to the point where they can build and deliver a new PC to the customer's doorstep in fewer than seven business days. Their supply webs are lean to the point of having only a few days of inventory, and both companies operate with *negative* working capital. They collect the buyer's money *before* they pay for the components that go to the machine.

Other manufacturing industries can and *must* move in the direction pioneered by Dell, Gateway, and Amazon. This won't be easy, especially for industries such as auto and aircraft, whose products are an order of magnitude more complex than anything Dell has to deal with. But it will happen. The Internet is changing how consumers interact with dealers, manufacturers, and even the products they buy. Today's supply chains are being replaced by electronically connected, integrated Value Webs that link all information, processes, and people—from the online consumer to a far-flung Tier-Two supplier. Entirely new levels of customization, speed, and cost reduction are now possible.

Appendix A of this book, "The Concept Automotive Industry Project," represents one view of how the world of automobile design, marketing, and manufacturing may look in the not-too-distant future.

Chapter 8

Managing and Applying Knowledge

Knowledge is both raw material and finished goods in today's corporations.

Dorothy Leonard
Wellsprings of Knowledge

Knowledge has always been a key ingredient of economic production, although we are only now appreciating its importance. Years ago, economists liked to say that all wealth was based on some combination of natural resources, capital, and labor. We now understand that these three factors produced nothing unless they were leavened with a healthy dose of knowledge of how things worked and what customers would buy. Agrarian societies needed not only seeds, land, and labor but also knowledge about when to plant, how to cultivate, when to harvest, and how to store and distribute their crops. Knowledge became even more critical in Industrial Age production as science assumed a larger role in human enterprise.

Today, the role of knowledge in value creation is immense and growing larger by the year, if the number of people employed in information-based sectors of the economy is any indication. In many industrial fields—automobiles and computers being good examples—the material content of products relative to their utility is growing smaller and smaller. Meanwhile, the informational or knowledge content of these products grows apace. For firms such as our own, Ernst & Young, knowledge in the form of solutions to business problems and challenges is the actual output of production. The same is true for just about every consulting company and for entire departments of most industrial companies—design, engineering, and R&D being notable examples. For all companies, knowledge is a critical enabler of product and process innovation and operational excellence.

Knowledge is also an enabler of innovation. As our colleague Rudy Ruggles has written, "Product innovations are the result of a group's knowledge of unserved markets and/or new technical possibilities."[1] In this he is absolutely correct. Product innovations do not appear out of the blue, but emerge from what people know about human needs and current or potential materials or technologies. When Honda engineers were initially faced in the early 1970s with a new U.S. statutory requirement to either (1) install catalytic converters, (2) develop a cleaner-burning engine, or (3) exit the U.S. automobile market, they marshaled their knowledge of engine design to develop an engine capable of meeting the legal standard. The need was there in black and white. So too were bits and pieces of accumulated knowledge that, when combined with newly generated knowledge, created a breakthrough solution: the CVCC (Compound Vortex Controlled Combustion) engine. The CVCC was so clean-burning that it met U.S. emissions standards without a catalytic converter, an innovation that Honda's rivals claimed could not be done.

The most stunning innovations often occur when knowledge from different and generally separate sources are brought together in creative ways. Perhaps the greatest proof of this statement could be found in the U.S. Apollo program, which landed a team of astronauts on the surface of the moon in July 1969 and brought them safely home. The Apollo crew rode into space on a NASA rocket, but the power that truly propelled their voyage was accumulated knowledge drawn from many diverse fields: astronomy, chemistry, physics, metallurgy, human physiology, electronics, telecommunications, computing, aerospace engineering, and project management. In this sense, the Apollo crew stood squarely on the shoulders of past discoverers. Knowledge gained and utilized from previous flights was equally important. It is doubtful that the mission would have succeeded had the Apollo program failed to tap any one of these storehouses of human understanding.

The Apollo program and its very public competition with the Soviets is a metaphor for role of knowledge in the realm of commercial competition. As Harvard's Dorothy Leonard has written, "Companies, like individuals, compete on the basis of their ability to create and utilize knowledge."[2] The same can be said for alliances and supply chains formed from many companies. At bottom, commercial competition today can be viewed as one set of knowledge and operational know-how pitted against another.

Given the competitive importance of knowledge, it follows that organizations should create, capture, and manage knowledge with the same dedication they bring to managing capital, human resources, and production. That fact has not been lost on forward thinking corporations, and most are now creating formal programs of knowledge management.

Knowledge management (KM) is a systematic approach to capturing knowledge, storing that knowledge in ways that make it easily accessible, and reusing knowledge. Its goal is to strengthen or revitalize an organization's core and enabling competencies.

A complete KM system deals with both the *explict* and the *tacit* knowledge of its employees. Explicit knowledge takes the form of reports, data, and other information—things that can be captured, codified, and shared directly, especially

SOME DEFINITIONS

Any discussion of KM involves important terms that are often tossed around indiscriminately. In this chapter, we have adopted the American Production Quality Center's (APQC) definitions of these terms:

Intellectual capital. The commercial value of trademarks, licenses, brand names, etc.

Data. Facts and figures without context or interpretation.

Information. Data in context or data interpreted (as in patterns).

Knowledge. Information in action.

Source: Carla O'Dell and C. Jackson Grayson, Jr., *If Only We Knew What We Know* (New York: Free Press, 1998), 4–5.

through information technology. Current inventories, this quarter's financial reports, studies, and historical data on equipment downtime are examples of explicit knowledge. Tacit knowledge is more subtle but every bit as important. Tacit knowledge is what exists in the heads of employees: an unrecorded recollection about how a production breakdown was quickly remedied; a salesperson's knowledge of the behavior of certain customers and competitors; the subtle wisdom imparted from a mentor to a younger employee. Tacit knowledge is the institutional memory we seek out and use every day. One of the unanticipated consequences of the downsizing binge of the pervious decade was the loss of tacit knowledge and institutional memory—something that the headcount-cutters only noticed after the fact. While it is difficult to deal with, steps can be taken to codify, store, or share tacit knowledge more effectively. At Ernst & Young, our service and industry teams share tacit knowledge through periodic forums where they discuss "lessons learned," best

RESHAPING THE CORPORATION WITH KNOWLEDGE

"Companies survive on their ability to adapt when necessary, and it is increasingly necessary for them to do so. . . . Successful adaptation seems to involve the thoughtful, incremental redirection of skills and knowledge bases so that today's expertise is reshaped into tomorrow's capabilities" (Leonard, *Wellsprings,* xi). Monsanto is a major corporation that has reshaped itself and the knowledge base on which it competes. Over a period of 15 years, Monsanto has strategically migrated from the domain of mainline chemical producers to its current focus on bioengineer products. There is a similar pattern of strategic adaptation in several auto supply companies.

practices, and so on. Managers of these forums are charged with picking up and recording the threads of these discussions and using them to help develop white papers and thought leadership that other employees can use with clients.

A particular firm may have strategic reasons for giving greater attention to one form of knowledge over the other. In either case, a good KM system is dynamic, recognizing, as Dorothy Leonard has written, that "knowledge accumulates slowly, over time, shaped and channels into certain directions through the nudging of hundreds of daily managerial decisions; [and] it is constantly aborning."[3]

■ THE KNOWLEDGE PROCESS

Our understanding of knowledge has changed considerable over the past decade. Where once we viewed knowledge as something we controlled and periodically invigorated with new knowledge, we now recognize knowledge as a continuing process of generation, storage, application, and learning (Figure 8.1). Our storehouse of knowledge grows as we create new knowledge through R&D and capture it from external sources and learning. Effective knowledge management adds value to stored knowledge by combining related elements and by making it easily retrievable. That stored knowledge can then be applied or reused to create value for customers. And what we learn in this last step adds to our knowledge storehouse.

➤ Capturing and Generating Knowledge

If an organization is to strengthen and/or revitalize its core and enabling capabilities, it must identify and capture the knowledge it needs. As Figure 8.2 illustrates, this vital knowledge may be external to the firm or it may be found internally. It may be generated through research and development. Whichever the case, once it enters the knowledge management system, it can be used to strengthen organizational capabilities.

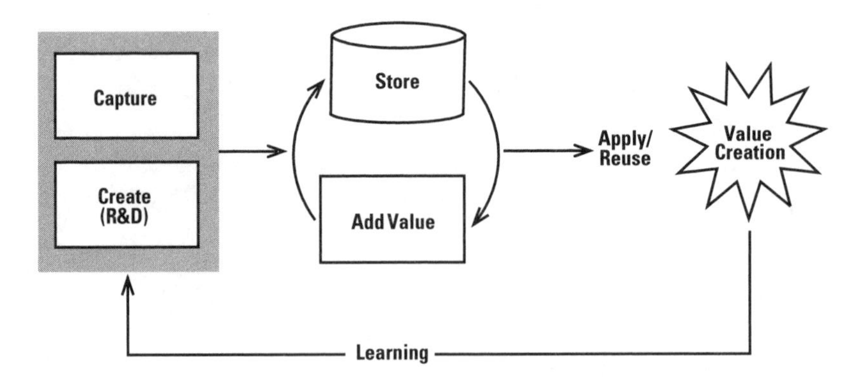

Figure 8.1 The knowledge process.

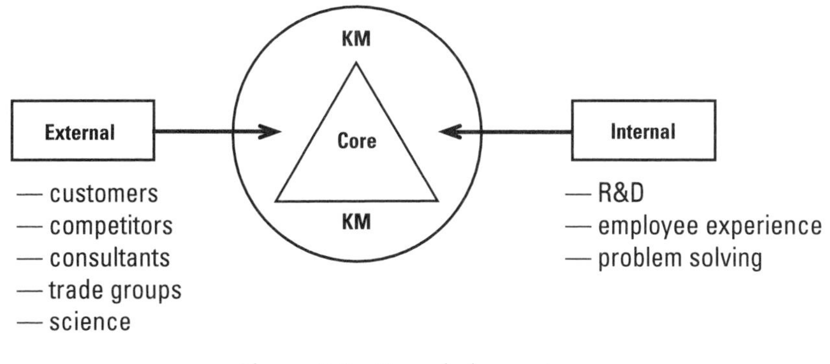

Figure 8.2 Knowledge capture.

External knowledge may be captured through employee education or by simply acquiring people or companies with experience and know-how. Delphi Saginaw Steering began a process of knowledge capture once its head of engineering received the official go-ahead to develop electronic-assisted steering, which required knowledge and skills then total absent within the company. Dana Corporation did the same once it understood its own need to develop capabilities in the area of suspension design. Dana's first move in acquiring that capability was to hire an engineer with 10 years of suspension experience. That individual headed up the new suspension area and began a long period of development, which involved the training of Dana employees. In other situations, Dana has turned to acquisition to capture the technical knowledge it needed for implementing corporate level strategy. Joint ventures or other partnering form can often accomplish the same goal.

For many large, multidivisional companies, the challenge of knowledge capture is to round up the knowledge that is already inside the organization but tucked away in ways that make it invisible or difficult to share. This knowledge can be substantial and hugely valuable. Carla O'Dell and C. Jackson Greyson, Jr. of APQC report, "Texas Instruments generated

$1.5 billion in annual increased fabrication capacity (in effect, a 'free' plant) by comparing and transferring best practices among its existing thirteen fabrication plants."[4] Likewise, Chevron learned that it could reduce operating costs by at least $20 million each year by identifying and adopting practices already used by its best-managed field. Cases like this one are not unique. Our own firm's revenues have been growing at a 20 percent annual rate in large measure because Ernst & Young has institutionalized the capture and reuse of internally generated knowledge. For a people-intensive business like ours, this makes it possible to expand revenues at a faster rate than people costs.

➤ Benchmarking

Benchmarking is a powerful tool of knowledge management. It first burst onto the scene in the late 1980s, producing a bumper crop of books and consulting services. But this great tool was not entirely new.

Bill Klann worked as a foreman in Henry Ford's Model T engine assembly plant. Like others in the early Ford organization, he was under pressure to find ways of speeding the assembly process. And since the moving assembly line as we've come to know it did not yet exist in the world of manufacturing, there was plenty of room for discovery and improvement.

One day in 1913, Klann and some colleagues decided to visit a slaughterhouse in the Detroit area on the chance that they might learn something that could be applied to the auto assembly business. Cattle and hog slaughtering was a *dis*assembly business, but Klann and his colleagues were nevertheless impressed by what they saw, particularly by the use of conveyers in speeding up the disassembly process.

Klann took the idea back to the Ford plant and began experimenting with the use of a conveyor in the assembly of one component of the Model T engine.[5] Industrial historians often point to this application as the beginning of the modern assembly line. It was also an early application of a process improvement concept that we now call "benchmarking."

Benchmarking, as defined by the APQC, is a process of measuring and comparing an organization's business processes against those of business process leaders anywhere in the world. The aim is to gain information that will help the organization improve its performance. In this sense, it represents an important method of knowledge capture. The story about Bill Klann indicates how benchmarking can be used to capture ideas and knowledge generated outside the firm. The same methods can be—and often are—used to identify and capture best practices and knowledge found inside large, decentralized organizations. As cited in Carla O'Dell's and C. Jackson Greyson's excellent book, Texas Instruments used internal benchmarking to identify practices in one operation and transfer them to others. "We had pockets of mediocrity right next door to world-class performance simply because one operation did not know what was happening at the other operation," explained Cindy Johnson, director of TI's Collaboration and Knowledge Sharing.[6]

➤ Storing Knowledge

People have been storing knowledge for as long as they have had writing and oral traditions. In the past, books and manuals have been the medium of choice for knowledge storage. This medium is fast giving way to digital storage in networked information systems. These systems have important advantages; digitally stored information can be:

- ➤ Rapidly distributed and retrieved.
- ➤ Easily updated.
- ➤ Arrayed or organized in more useful ways.

In the knowledge management business, this type of storage is often referred to as "codifying." Codifying is most applicable to explicit knowledge.

Tom Davenport described a case of stored codified knowledge in a recent issue of our *Perspectives on Business Innovation.*[7] In this case, an "information technical engineer" at Hewlett-Packard has begun developing an internal database guide to human knowledge resources within HPs decentralized laboratories. It is designed to answer a complaint that "If only HP knew what HP knows." The primary content of its database is a set of expert "profiles" of HP experts on different technical topics. Once the database is complete and available, any HP engineer or scientist will be able to search for an internal expert on a particular subject using familiar search engine approaches.

Another HP initiative aims to solve a similar problem for the company's 2,000 educator/trainers. They had complained that they "didn't know what was going on." To solve this problem, Bruce Karney, a member of HP's Corporate Education organization, set to work to codify the company's diverse training materials, make them available electronically, and provide a medium through which trainers and educators could contribute and discuss their materials and methods. Using Lotus Notes™ as the medium, Karney created two different knowledge bases: a "Trainer's Trading Post" where employees could contribute their own ideas and respond to others; and a Training Library, a collection of HP training documents.

In this same spirit of codifying what is already known, a small team at DaimlerChrysler has created a system and process for sharing knowledge quickly across teams and divisions. The centerpiece of the system comprises DaimlerChrysler's "Engineering Books of Knowledge" (EBOKs). EBOKs are a combination of Lotus Notes database repositories and discussion forums containing "lessons learned" in context and "best practices" information focused for use within the engineering community. Why EBOKs? DaimlerChrysler already had community of interest forums called "Tech Clubs," which focused on specific technologies and engineering issues. But the sharing of information at the Tech Clubs resulted in varying levels of success. The company needed a new way to capture the expert knowledge of its people, increase engineering efficiency, reduce product development time, improve product quality, and avoid repeating earlier mistakes. EBOKs were created to serve this purpose. Each EBOK is sponsored by one of the eleven Executive Tech Clubs, which are responsible for identifying sections, assigning authors/owners, and reviewing content. To-date, over 5,000 DaimlerChrysler engineers use EBOKs with about half of this population also contributing as authors, reviewers, or book owners.

The DaimlerChrysler EBOKs are part of a larger knowledge management system that aims to enhance the company's competitive position through application of leading edge knowledge management processes and technologies throughout DaimlerChrysler and its extended enterprise. That "extended enterprise" includes many of the suppliers with which the company works in a partnership way. The sharing is in fact mutual, since a corresponding Supplier Book of Knowledge (SBOK) is made available to DaimlerChrysler personnel (Figure 8.3).

➤ Applying and Reusing Knowledge

A big payback of KM is the ability to apply or reuse knowledge gained in the past or in another operation. At Ernst & Young, many of our consultants are engaged in installing enterprise resource planning systems—huge, integrated software systems—and training people to use them effectively. This is detailed and often tedious work. So when one of our

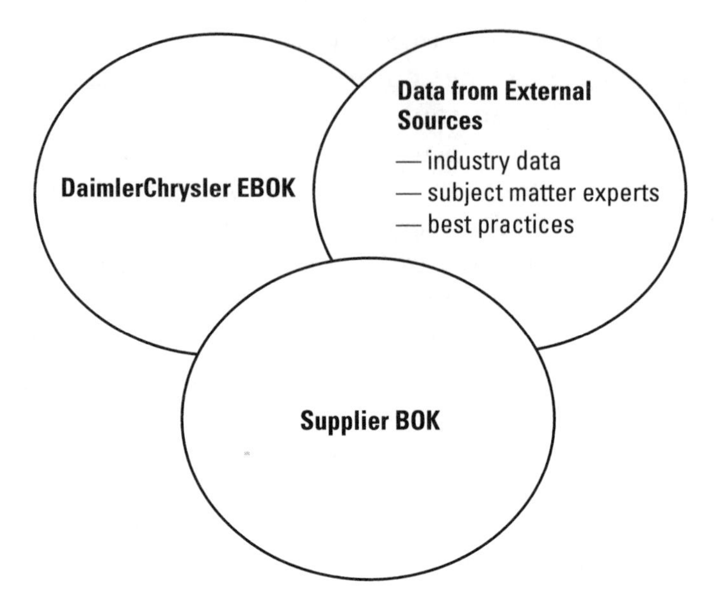

Figure 8.3 Knowledge sharing at DaimlerChrysler.

people finishes an engagement in a particular area, we develop interview guides, work schedules, benchmark data, and so on, and codify them electronically so that other Ernst & Young personnel encountering analogous situations can avoid reinventing the same wheel. They can save time and effort by retrieving and using the stored data in ways that save them time and effort. This increases the productivity of expensive personnel and creates customer satisfaction.

Perhaps 60 percent of the knowledge we try to manage in our own firm can be codified in print and digital form using a "people-to-documents" approach. Information is extracted from the individuals who develop it, made independent of those individuals and their clients, and made available for reuse. Here, the union of knowledge management and information technology is a marriage made in heaven. The remaining 40 percent or so, however, involves tacit knowledge. What we hope to do with tacit knowledge is to identify it and

BRICKS AND MORTAR MATTER

One aspect of knowledge management often overlooked in the current literature and practice is the spatial relationship of individuals and functions. Take a look at your own office layout. Is it the typical long corridor with closed, private offices along each side? Are workspaces arranged by organizational pecking order? Are encounters with important coworkers infrequent or must they be planned in advance? If you answered "yes" to any of these questions, you are working in a traditional spatial arrangement that is generally nonconducive to knowledge sharing.

Organizations are just beginning to understand how spatial relationships affect knowledge sharing. Our own company's experiment with this issue is the Ernst & Young Center for Business Innovation, located in Cambridge, Massachusetts. There, everything from office spaces, the application of information technology, and the use of meeting spaces has been designed to facilitate frequent communications, knowledge sharing, and collaborative problem-solving.

DaimlerChrysler Corporation had the same concept in mind when it designed and built its $1.1 billion Technology Center in Auburn Hills, Michigan. This megastructure (finished in 1993) brought approximately 10,500 employees from almost every discipline under one roof to develop cars and trucks using the company's platform team concept. All the disciplines required for planning, developing, and selling a new product—engineering, design, manufacturing, procurement and supply, and corporate staffs, including sales, marketing, and finance—share this 4.4 million-square-foot facility. Proximity and open lines of sight and communications facilitate joint effort and knowledge sharing. BMW accomplished something very similar when it created Europe's largest research engineering center, the Fiz Center. Located in Munich, the Fiz Center's series of towers and connecting hallways keep almost 6,000 engineers and designers in close contact. By design, the maximum walking distance between any two individuals is 150 meters. Some estimate that spatial relationships created by the Fiz Center have helped BMW slash its product development time by nearly two years.

LEARNING LESSONS

When the first Armored Division was shipped to Bosnia in the mid-1990s as a peace-keeping force, a team from the U.S. Army's Center for Army Lessons Learned (CALL) went with it. As separate units of officers and enlisted men figured out how to deal with the terrain and the various opposing and civilian groups, CALL personnel collected the "lessons learned" and quickly disseminated them to other units.

The Bosnian experience is just one of the latest in a long series of conflicts studied by this special Army unit. CALL, which is based at Fort Leavenworth, Kansas, collects and analyzes data from current and historical sources, including Army operations and training events, and transfers its information to U.S. military personnel via print and electronic media.

transfer it to others it could benefit. Traditional means of communication are often the best approaches to transferring tacit knowledge. Brainstorming, meetings, electronic chat rooms, and "communities of interest" are among the methods companies now use to encourage that transfer.

■ KNOWLEDGE MANAGEMENT AND INNOVATION

Innovation is one of the intended payoffs of knowledge management. Many innovations in industry are sparked when two or more bits of information come together. A customer describes a vexing problem to a service engineer who is aware of a new technology in search of an application. A scientist in the R&D lab of one division compares notes with a scientist working in another division on a similar problem. One company saved millions in the development of items like pumps and construction materials when it instituted a system for bringing together once-separate pieces of information within its worldwide engineering operations.

Like pieces in a jigsaw puzzle, isolated bits of information that seem devoid of meaning can provide the outlines of a coherent insight when brought together. The failure of organizations to bring together bits of information already captured in separate functional silos wastes time and slows down everything. We know, for example, that engineers working for one U.S. automaker spend the equivalent of *one day each week* simply looking for information. No organization can afford to waste that amount of engineering staff time. In many cases, the information these engineers spend their time hunting down is eventually found inside the company—buried in a file drawer or obscure database, or in somebody's head. A good knowledge management system does two things to eliminate this waste:

1. It provides a process for capturing the information its engineers need.
2. It stores the information in a highly accessible form.

➤ Communities of Interest

Codifiable knowledge is important to innovators. Used effectively, it can save them time and money. A "who knows what?" database (or "pointer system") like the one being developed at Hewlett-Packard can quickly tell researchers and engineers whom to call when they need information or verification of their own ideas. But the knowledge with the greatest potential value to innovators is generally stored between the ears of fellow scientists, salespeople, and customers as tacit knowledge.

The best way to get at this tacit knowledge is through "communities of interest" (COINs)—a network of individuals who share a common task or technical interest. The network facilitates communication and, by extension, knowledge sharing. According to our colleague, Ralph Poole:

> *COINs provide opportunities to debate the merits of experiences and to identify learnings that we can organize and transfer. At Ernst & Young, COINs are where most innovations happen. People get together to share their problem solving experiences. They can identify the most effective and ground-breaking solutions. These are then transferred quickly around the company.*

Here are a few examples of COINs in action:

- Every operating unit of Xerox has one or more benchmarking specialists. Depending on the unit's size, benchmarking may be a full- or part-time job for these individuals. Though they are separated widely in the Xerox universe, these individuals form a community of interest.
- Chevron has a network of 100 people whose common interest is to find more efficient approaches to the company's own use of energy.
- 3M has communities and subcommunities of interest associated with each of its core technical competencies. These people are brought together at regular intervals to share information and to hear the ideas of outside experts brought in to give seminars or speeches.

COINs can *and should* extend beyond corporate borders to include interested parties in other organizations. The Xerox benchmarkers, for example, are part of a larger community of interest that spans companies in different industries. This makes it possible for any individual in the COIN to obtain information about benchmarking "targets" located in unaffiliated industries.

When people in COINs work in isolation from one another, companies must find ways in which they can regularly interact and share the information and ideas that so often result in new insights and practical innovations. In practice, these include:

- Newsletters.
- Periodic meetings or forums.
- Chat-room type electronic connections and groupware such as Lotus Notes.

➤ Obstacles

Most practitioners of KM point to organizational culture as the greatest obstacle to capturing, storing, and sharing information. When company functions behave like "silos," they may be able to create and share knowledge within the vertical structure of their silos, but they will resist sharing with other units. The same behavior is observable at the individual level. When people are valued and rewarded for their technical expertise or specific knowledge, they may be less likely to share what they know. Doing so might diminish their value to the organization. Bechtel's Richard Armstrong pointed to this issue in describing his company's first attempt to develop a system of KM. "We didn't stop to wonder: why would someone whose personal marketability depends on their knowledge and productivity take time out from a busy day to make what they know widely available?"[8]

Time and money create another obstacle to effective knowledge management. If people do not have slack time in which to attend networking meetings and the travel budgets that permit visits to other facilities and professional conferences, active network sharing will not take place. Likewise, if people experience no rewards for the time they take from their regular work to participate in knowledge sharing, they are unlikely to do it.

➤ Performance Metrics

Like every "good idea," knowledge management adds costs to business operations—for information hardware and software, for the considerable time employees must take to store and/or share what they have learned with others, and for KM managers. Given these costs, KM must demonstrate improved results. Traditional cost/benefit analysis is nearly impossible to apply to KM. However, senior managers can gauge the cost-effectiveness of their knowledge management efforts using process and "results" metrics like the following Ernst & Young metrics:

Process Metrics	*Results Metrics*
Amount of reusable content.	Value creation.
Participation levels (usage).	Thought (innovation) leadership.
Input cycle time.	Customer satisfaction.

■ KM AND YOUR COMPANY

Innovation is more likely to occur in an organization that is continually recharging its storehouse of information and knowledge. Where does your company stand in terms of "knowing what it already knows" and its ability to capture, store, and reuse knowledge? Are people in one unit spending time and effort to learn what employees in another unit already know? Are the best practices developed in one location quickly made available to others? Are your people tapped into the outside world of information and ideas? Does your organization support communities of interest for diffusing information and knowledge? Do people know whom to call when they need information? When someone quits or retires, is there an observable loss of organizational knowledge or memory?

If you cannot respond positively to these questions, start thinking about a program of knowledge management. As you do so, consider these issues:

- The *type* of knowledge that will most benefit your organization. It may be knowledge that's unique to a particular set of problems (e.g., engineering data), or it may be generally applicable knowledge (e.g., a decision-making process). Focus on the type of knowledge that directly serves your business strategy.
- The *degree* to which the knowledge you need is codifiable; this will determine the appropriate KM mechanisms (e.g., a database for highly codifiable knowledge; a COIN for tacit knowledge).
- Don't be tempted by a "technical fix." Millions spent on information systems will not guarantee effective knowledge management.

Chapter 9

Leading the Race toward Innovation

When you know that innovation is the key to the future, you can afford to take some risks.

Brian Koop

Each of the preceding chapters has described one or more aspects of innovation. What we've saved for last is the role of leadership in creating and sustaining innovation. Much of what we have to say on leadership is directed to senior executives who, more than others, have direct responsibility for choosing strategic direction, developing the internal policies that either nourish or starve innovation, aligning the resources, and motivating the people. But because leadership is needed at all levels, this chapter speaks to every reader.

■ LEADING FROM THE TOP

One of the important lessons of our PACE studies is that innovation can be either top down or bottom up. Some ideas—

generally strategic—are conceived and driven from the top. Some come from customers; and still others percolate up from bench scientists and other personnel further down in the organization.

The development of fiber optics by Corning is a classic case of innovation driven from the top. As told by Joseph Morone,[1] then-CEO William Armistead received a report from one of his researchers in 1966 indicating that the British Post Office (which operated the nation's telephone system at the time) wanted Corning to investigate the development of glass fibers as a means of transmitting telecommunications signals. Corning already had some experience with these fibers, and was selling some as "light pipes" to illuminate automobile dashboard instruments. But this was a tiny market, and there was no indication that these fibers could handle electronic signals. Nevertheless, Armistead saw the kernel of a good idea and put his weight behind it:

> *I could see that if you could really solve this thing it had some merit in it. I didn't dream what it would turn out to be, or how big it might be, but anyway, it looked like an intriguing idea, and I said, "Why don't we solve it?*[2]

Armistead's endorsement of a fiber-optics project turned out to have strategic importance for Corning, though he clearly didn't recognize it at the time.

The development of E-Steer at Delphi Saginaw was likewise viewed as strategic from the very beginning, and provides another case of innovation driven from the top. In that instance, high-level executives with their thumbs on the pulse of industry change identified a compelling opportunity—in the broad sense—and used their authority to refocus the technical trajectory of the company. Don Runkle,

Paul Tosch, and Aly Badawy could see how the wave of electronics was washing over the entire automotive industry and recognized two choices: ride the wave, or be washed away by it.

In hindsight, the decision made by Delphi executives appears to be simple, but it was anything but simple at the time. The Saginaw Steering division was a leader in its field but had no competencies in the new technology. Even the appointed leader of this initiative lacked background in electronics. With a PhD in mechanical engineering, his skills were better suited to the company's traditional business. Nevertheless, it became his task to build competency in the new technology, which he did through targeted recruiting from companies like Hughes Aircraft and Black & Decker, eventually assembling a nonmechanical engineering talent pool that included 20 PhDs.

Resistance was also an issue that challenged the leadership. The E-Steer project encountered resistance from people whose skills and careers were closely associated with hydraulic assisted steering. But, as one company executive told us, "There was plenty of work for our mechanical engineers to do" in the traditional business, which continued to grow despite market beachheads established by E-Steer. In fact, the two technological cultures within Delphi Saginaw now appear to coexist happily, and at this writing are collaborating on a hybrid (hydraulic-electric) steering system for the Opel Astra.

We could hypothesize that top-down innovation is the surest approach for moving a company from one generation of technology to another, as happened in both the Corning and Delphi cases. "Without the commitment of our leadership," the head of engineering told us, "I can guarantee that we would have failed miserably. The leadership was committed to our taking [this technology] to the limit."

UP FROM THE BOTTOM

Innovation from the top is rare, excepting two cases: start-up companies, where the founder is also the key idea generator; and situations in which everyone understands that the company must change or die. In the vast majority of cases, ideas are generated much lower in the organization and must appeal upward for approval and support.

This process of idea generation was described in Chapter 2. It depends for success on a "recognizer," a person who see the value of the idea, encourages its development, and helps the innovator connect with sources of support. That support may be unofficial or official. Unofficial support takes the form of "bootlegging" familiar to research scientists. Official support usually comes from the company's formal funding mechanism—either an internal venture board, or a stage-gate system of review and approval.

Though most innovation is bottom up, senior executives nevertheless have a critical role to play in the process. They can:

- Provide strategic direction to innovators by providing boundaries within which innovations should be focused.
- Align the resources with promising new ideas.
- Encourage and shape projects through early stage involvement.
- Develop mechanisms that encourage innovation.

➤ Strategic Direction

Innovators must have some strategic boundaries within which they can feel free to generate ideas. Strategic boundaries help innovators to focus on developments that are feasible for the company. Lacking these boundaries, they can waste a great deal of time and effort.

How many times have your company's R&D personnel pushed an innovative project along for months, only to be told: "It's a great idea, but not for us." Not every good idea makes sense for a particular company, if only because the company lacks the manufacturing or customer base to make the most of it. Good management reduces the chance of wasting time on inappropriate concepts by making sure that everyone understands the strategic goals of the company and the boundaries within which ideas should be developed.

The companies that we observe to sustain innovation generally excel within the boundaries of well-defined, high-payoff central competencies. They are just as clear on what to stay out of as what to go into. These companies focus R&D investments in areas where they can add the greatest value, and they stay out of others. Says Gentex's Fred Bauer:

> *I tell people that the greatest chance of success comes when we're dealing from strength, from processes and technologies that we know and understand, and from dealing with customers we know and understand. This doesn't mean that we shouldn't try to develop ideas outside those core competencies, it just means that any such new idea must be much better the further it gets away from the core. We reinforce this notion on a day-to-day basis. An idea will come up and we'll say, "Yes, but we don't have any marketing there," or "We don't understand that technology." We teach this through what we do day in and day out, by what we talk about, so that it becomes intuitive for employees. The kinds of people we hire also determines the direction of the ideas that come up.*

Other companies use formal programs to determine the strategic direction and communicate that direction to employees. Dana Corporation's Technology Roundtable, first described in Chapter 6, provides a good example. Based on discussions with customers and its own engineers, Roundtable members identify opportunities and key technologies about which more needs to be known. A group of "scanners" then seek out information on these technologies and their potential application. This information is then brought back to the Technology board where decisions are made on next steps, resource allocation, and possible applications. The Motorola Roadmap Program is another example of how a company can provide high-level strategic direction.

Having said this, we must remember that strategy and innovation should be intertwined. Each should be allowed to influence the other (Figure 9.1). Strategy should give direction to those who pursue innovation, but a breakthrough with the potential to create enormous value for shareholders should never be discouraged or dismissed simply because it would force a change in strategic direction. Strategy, after all, is the servant of shareholders, and must bend to their best interests.

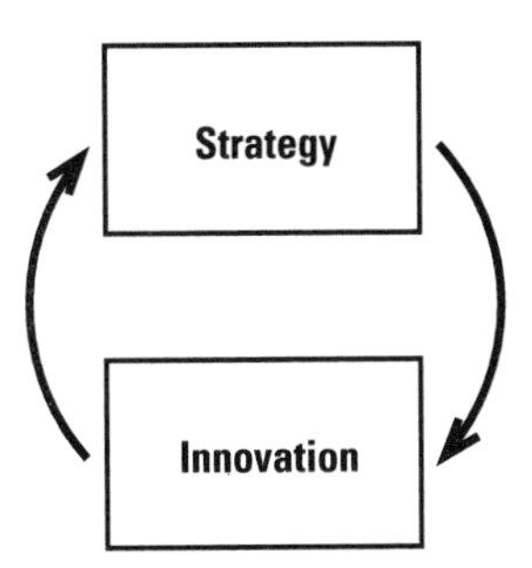

Figure 9.1 The strategy-innovation linkage.

■ THE EXECUTIVE ROLE

Except in small companies, senior corporate leaders are rarely part of the bottom-up course of innovation. By the time that most executives get involved with these projects, half the work is already done. Many report that they spend very little of their time working with early-stage development of product or process innovations, and this is supported by academic findings. Even those who would like to be more involved with early-stage work find their time eaten up by personnel issues, budgeting, conflict resolution, investor relations, and travel. The time they do give to development projects usually occurs very late in the game, when their influence has the *least* impact on the form or direction of the innovation.

Steven Wheelwright and Kim Clark have studied when and how often senior managers intervened in product development projects. A map of their findings is represented in Figure 9.2.

As indicated, the greatest opportunities for senior managers to influence these projects come early on, in the knowledge acquisition and concept investigation stages—when most executives are notably absent. In the Wheelwright/Clark finding, these executives only make their presence known very late in the game, during prototype building and ramp-up, when their influence on projects is negligible. "It is our experience that senior managers' ability to influence the outcome of development activities rarely coincides with where and when they actually focus their attention."[3] These findings suggest a redirection of executive leadership: taking a more active role in early-stage development, including the front end of the stage-gate review system.

If you are a senior executive, you need to be visibly involved in the generation and nurturing of innovation. One

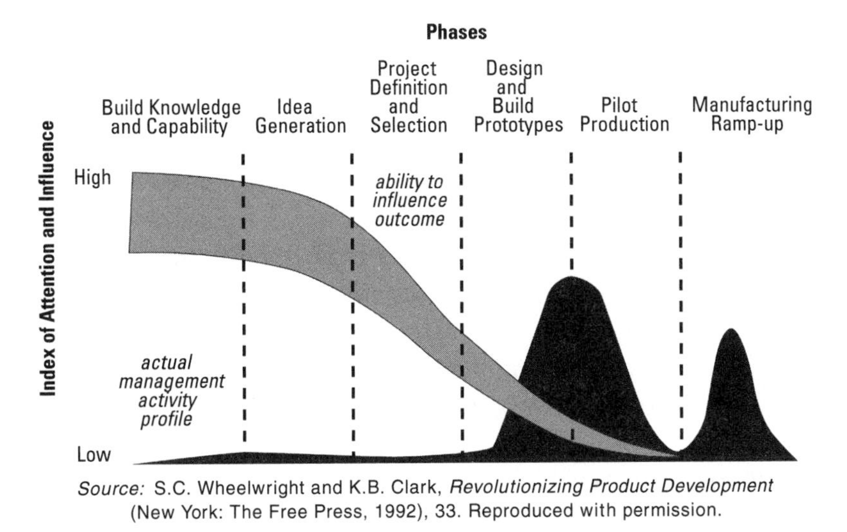

Source: S.C. Wheelwright and K.B. Clark, *Revolutionizing Product Development* (New York: The Free Press, 1992), 33. Reproduced with permission.

Figure 9.2 Senior management involvement in development projects: Too often too late.

of the best ways to do this is to be a regular visitor to your engineering and R&D labs. These are the birthing rooms of your company future. Spending time with these employees will do three important things:

1. It will send a signal that senior management thinks engineering and R&D are vital to the company.
2. It will keep you in touch with the technical possibilities and constraints faced by the organization; this will make you a better decision maker.
3. You'll be energized from these associations. "I've always visited the labs," Robert Galvin wrote in describing his years at Motorola. "In the '60s I prowled them. It was fun. It was the best way to learn by osmosis some of the engineering so well known by many of our best people."[4]

Even when they cannot or will not drive innovation from the top, senior managers can do a number of things to encourage innovation and assure that the ideas that come up from below have the potential to move the company in ways it should go.

Several earlier chapters of this book identified organizational issues that have a direct bearing on the ability of any company to innovate on a sustained basis: an innovation-friendly environment; development of employee skills, and the capture, storage, and application of knowledge. Within those larger frameworks, here are a few action steps we've learned from our clients that any corporate executive can take to encourage innovation.

➤ Create Many Alternative Paths Forward

Would you entrust all your company's decisions on new product ideas to a single technical person or manager? Probably not. No single person has the insight to recognize value in every idea that comes along. Virtually every senior scientist and executive can point to a "big one" that got away because he or she failed to recognize its potential impact. Nevertheless, a specific individual or a single review committee generally determines the fate of ideas that percolate out of R&D centers and other sources. If that single gateway fails to open, the idea goes nowhere and the individual innovator is discouraged. Within your own framework of resource limitations, try to create multiple paths along which projects can continue moving. That way, if one is closed off—for any reason—the idea has some recourse. Many companies, including 3M, have formalized this system with courts of appeal. If a scientist or engineer can't get his or her direct supervisor's backing, he or she can appeal to a higher authority without recrimination.

➤ Look for Opportunities to Say "Yes"

We learned this one from Fred Bauer. "Part of being a good manager is being selective," he says, "but knocking down people's suggestions really trashes the spirit of guys who are trying to come up with new ideas. This is particularly true when ideas are blocked at the executive level. [Innovators] have had to run a gauntlet of bureaucracy to get that far." Instead of finding ways to say no, Bauer always looks for a reason to say yes. And, in his experience, these usually pay off. Even with a small company of 1,400 employees, he admits to not fully understanding many of the projects that come his way. "But my natural inclination is to say 'yes' instead of 'no.' I probably approve 95 percent of the capital project ideas that make it to me as a way of encouraging people. Fortunately, if you have the right culture in place, people won't bring up impractical ideas."

➤ Be Willing to Pay for Innovation

JCI's VP of Marketing, Mike Suman has reminded us that an innovative culture begins at the top. "It has to start at the top. John Barth, Rande Somma, and Mike Johnston are entirely committed to it." These executives budget for innovation—they provide employees with the funds they need for the R&D, marketing, and brand building that create powerful new products and product lines. "Management can say that they support innovation," Suman says, "but unless they vote with their dollars, they don't really mean it."

➤ Create a Partnership of Champions and Believers

Given the opportunity, people with good ideas attract other people who can help develop those ideas, improve them, and generate enthusiasm in the organization and with the right customers. These are high-spirited partnerships you need to energize your business. The worst thing you can do is throw cold water on these people. The best thing you can do is give them every opportunity to work together and spread the news about their innovations.

➤ Cultivate the Art of Cheap Failures

Innovation eats up resources, even when promising ideas actually work. It's even worse when management cannot or will not pull the plug on projects that should be terminated. If you think that this is a problem peculiar to your firm, think again. It is almost impossible to find a large company that does not have a few projects that employees jokingly refer to as "the creatures that will not die."

We see and hear about many ideas that have been starved rather than shot. If there are times when starving an idea of funding is a better alternative, we can't think of one. Three negatives, however, are associated with this practice: (1) Leadership appears to be indecisive; (2) the short rations given to many back-burner projects add up, depriving resources from more strategically important activities; and (3) the author of the idea gets no feedback, has no idea how to improve the idea, doesn't know what boundary he or she has violated, and may soon cease to generate new ideas.

To make the most of limited resources, assume the risks of lots of cheap failures. This will put the Law of Large Numbers on your side and improve the odds of real success. Try many things, but agree in advance that they'll be cut off if they fail to meet certain clear criteria early in development (a clear application, a technical hurdle overcome, broad organizational support, etc.). Cutting off a project is never a death sentence in any case. Think of it as putting it "on the shelf" until something else happens (e.g., an enabling technology is developed elsewhere).

➤ Use Alliances When Necessary

Since many new products and processes bring together very different technologies, it often makes sense to partner with another entity that brings a critical missing element to the table: a customer market, an enabling technology, or a manufacturing process you lack. This can save development time and lower overall risk. Gentex and Johnson Controls formed such a partnership when they developed auto dimming mirrors with internal direction capabilities. Motorola is highly strategic in its partnerships, using them both to increase the pace of innovation and to provide a conduit to new industries. Its philosophy is to create linkages with the most innovative partners—companies that will continue to flourish in the years ahead, and create even more opportunities for collaboration with Motorola.

➤ Look beyond Current Ideas to Superior Alternatives

In their book, *The Smart Organization,* James and David Matheson describe a "dialogue decision process" that some companies now use to improve the quality of their R&D decisions.[5] A number of companies, including General Motors and SmithKline Beecham, have adopted this decision process, an important step of which is to actively seek out alternatives to choices already on the table and supported by competing champions. Multifunctional teams are assigned the task of objectively assessing the risks and potential returns of each alternative and the development of superior "hybrid" concepts that draw out the best of each idea.

➤ Get People to Look Outward

Left to their own devices, most people become inward looking, focusing on what they already know, and defining reality in terms of narrow and often limited experiences. "Most companies become introverted," Fred Bauer told us, "and that's a very destructive thing. It's comfortable and being introverted becomes a habit."

A dangerous myopia will infect your company unless you do something to encourage people to look outside to the larger world of customers, competitors, science and technology, and developments in other industries. What can you do? Here are a few ideas:

- Encourage your technical people to attend professional conferences.
- "Repot" people from one job to another on a regular basis.
- Send scientists and engineers on customer visits with your salespeople.
- "Lend" your best engineers to your best customers for a month or more—you'll be surprised and delighted by the number of ideas they bring back.

➤ Don't Use the Rearview Mirror to Guide Innovation

Innovation efforts must look toward the future and not be guided by what worked in the past. Because the past is so rich in facts and examples of success or failure, employees who aim to create the future—which has no facts—are often frustrated in their attempts to financially justify their ideas. Anyone can challenge sales numbers projected into the future from an innovation. A real leader, however, connects different thoughts, ideas, and facts in sketching broad outlines of the future and where to make investments. Former Daimler-Chrysler CEO Bob Lutz, for example, had no data to support his approval of the second sliding door on the minivan. None of the company's market research could confirm that it would excite customers, yet it was a big hit.

➤ Make the Most of Inevitable Failures

Failure is an inevitable companion of innovative pursuits. Clay Christensen found in his research that successful managers of innovation "planned to fail early and *inexpensively*. . . . They found that their markets generally coalesced through an iterative process of trial, learning, and trial again."[6]

If your company is not experiencing failed projects, it is probably too risk adverse—in which case it is failing itself and its shareholders.

So, if failures are inevitable, learn what you can from them through project postmortems, and avoid stigmatizing the employees associated with them. Give out a lighthearted "Golden Lemon" trophy for a project that failed, or a "Purple Thumb" award for an idea that simply couldn't get backing. These are ways of telling everyone that trying but failing is acceptable, and that the company will honor creative efforts whether they succeed or fail.

Finally, if innovation represents the future of your organization, you must be part of the process. "Wander around" as they do at Hewlett-Packard and see what employees are working on. Ask how you can help. Motivate them when they are discouraged, and challenge them when they are not.

You cannot be a bystander with respect to your company's R&D and product development. Instead, get into the fuzzy front end where you can feel the winds of the future and where you can learn, encourage, and provide a strategic voice. That is what leadership for innovation is about.

Winning the Innovation Race

What all the successful entrepreneurs I have met have in common is not a certain kind of personality but a commitment to the systematic practice of innovation.

Peter F. Drucker
The Discipline of Innovation

We observe this fact in every industry with which we have contact: companies that innovate on a sustained basis rise toward the top, creating high employee morale, opportunities for personal growth, substantial bonuses, and shareholder wealth. Companies that fail to innovate sink toward the bottom of the heap.

Remarkably, a number of large, established companies—Motorola, General Electric, Hewlett-Packard, Corning, and 3M being notable examples—have been able to sustain innovation over many decades and through several generations of management. Their continuing industry leadership belies the popular notion that innovation is the exclusive preserve of small, young companies.

The key to sustaining innovation is to innovate simultaneously in three dimensions: people, processes, and technology. Each dimension lends strength and support to the others, creating a solid building block for the success of the entire enterprise. Weakness in any one dimension weakens the whole.

Previous chapters of this book have shown how your company can innovate in each of these key dimensions and have provided examples of enterprises that are doing it extremely well. Enterprises that innovate on a sustained basis do the following things very well:

- Create an innovation-friendly environment.
- Find ways to enhance the potential of every employee.
- Use and continually improve their process for developing new products.
- Seek opportunities for process innovation.
- Keep on the leading edge of technology and indulge in "technofusion" whenever possible.
- Look for opportunities to innovate in the supply chain.
- Build an effective system of knowledge management.
- Provide executive leadership.

You and your company can do these things, too, if you have commitment, patience, and the collaboration of managers and employees.

Appendix A

The Concept Automotive Industry Project

THE CONNECTED CAR COMPANY*

Just as concept cars provide glimpses of the automobiles of the future, this publication examines how these vehicles could be envisioned, produced, and sold.

In other words, this is our look ahead at a concept automotive industry of the future.

That automotive industry, like most businesses, will be defined largely by three key characteristics:

- *Speed.* Speed is the compression of time. Modern society—including the automotive industry—continues to dramatically reduce the time requirements for tasks such

---

* This appendix is reprinted from *The Concept Automobile Industry Project,*

Acknowledgments. Parts of this work are based on the descriptions of the future in the innovative book, *BLUR: The Speed of Change in the Connected Economy* (Addison-Wesley, 1998) by Christopher Meyer, director, Ernst & Young Center for Business Innovation; and Stan Davis, research fellow at the Center for Business Innovation and independent author. Copyright © 1998 by Ernst & Young LLP. Lee A. Sage and Theodor D. Richman.

as product development, manufacturing, and personal communications.

It is possible to produce thousands of innovative, customized products virtually overnight, and global distribution networks can move almost anything to anywhere—by the next day.

In much the same way that mechanical engineers have found ways to minimize friction, time is less and less of a factor in whatever we do. Time is not a factor unless it is squandered, and then its cost is huge.

➤ *Connectivity.* The world is the network. Technology is bringing us what all the politicians and diplomats couldn't achieve: a world in which we can see, speak, and *collaborate* with everyone, anywhere, at any time.

Automotive suppliers, customers, sellers, buyers, vendors, employees, supervisors, and all computers are connecting to each other, and moving forward together. To be unconnected is to be left behind.

➤ *Intangible value.* In the connected economy, bricks and mortar are liabilities in the eyes of Wall Street. Owning the means of producing innovative products is far less important than having *access* to those means.

Conversely, people, knowledge, relationships, and brands are increasingly valuable. People must start appearing on CEOs' mental balance sheets as assets, not liabilities. Emotionally laden brand names, trust, and relationships also must be highly valued by an organization, because those factors help forge connections with customers and business partners.

This publication explores how these three concepts are likely to affect the operation and structure of the automotive industry in ways large and small. It offers "slice of life" vignettes of the key players in the supply network—consumers, dealers, manufacturers, and suppliers—three years from now.

THREE DAYS IN THE LIVES OF ...

The Car Buyers

May 16, 2002—6:45 P.M.

Paul Daniels, a 36-year-old office manager, walked into his family room. "Okay, let's do it." he told his wife, clapping his hands. Paul Jr. looked up expectantly from his Cyber-Galactic Gaucho Rats toys. Whenever Dad clapped hands and used that tone of voice, they were going someplace fun.

But the Daniels were about to buy a car.

And they knew exactly which one they wanted—a $38,000 GL2000. It was a hybrid-powered, luxury sport utility vehicle that would be built to order. Paul liked the numbers. He'd bragged to his coworkers, "It gets 60 mpg, city. Does zero to 60 in 6.5 seconds. It has 600 megs of RAM and runs on a 1,500 megahertz processor."

"Remember, Jan, we're getting the *Jerry Garcia* print interior," he said, sitting down at their PC-TV. With a feigned roll of her eyes, Jan Daniels sat down beside her husband.

The Daniels were purchasing the GL2000 because their current car was a clunker from the last century. No GPS. No heads-up TV. No upgradeability. Deplorable gas mileage. And it had an antique AM/FM/CD player in the dash.

As for the GL2000, it had been love at first ride. During a recent family vacation to Disneyland, they'd rented a GL2000 1.0—paying only $29 for a week-long rental, thanks to the automaker's subsidy. Eager to get potential buyers behind the wheel of its innovative product, the carmaker had recognized that rentals could serve as the ideal "test drives." What's more, when Paul paid his bill at the Avis-Hertz counter, he received collateral material and a voucher offering a $1,500 rebate that he was about to cash in.

"Internet . . . shopping . . . automotive," Paul now said to the PC-TV. The 56-inch, flat-screen display on the wall sprang to life.

The Internet connection took less than a second.

Paul spoke again.

"We want to buy a GL2000."

* * *

Just five blocks away, another car buyer, Aimee Nguyen wasn't only deciding *what* car to buy, she was wrestling with *how* to buy it.

She had a lot of options.

There were a half-dozen dealers within 10 miles—not that Aimee would have to leave her apartment. Over the past two years, the Internet had become one of the most popular methods for purchasing a new car. But there were plenty of other sales channels, too.

For example, the new QVAuto TV shopping channel offered both new and certified "renaissance" (reconditioned used) vehicles. Also there was Charles, a friend who automatically became a salesperson—and a zealous one—whenever he bought a particular brand of car. If all that wasn't enough, Aimee's parents had been pushing her to buy her car through their church group.

For a brief while Aimee had even toyed with the option suggested by her cousin Vinh—a "transportation contract" at a local dealer that would let her switch back and forth between various types of cars. "Think of it, Aimee," he'd told her. "A convertible in the summer. A four-wheel drive in the winter. A hot sports car you can drive to your 10-year high-school reunion." Appealing thought. But those $500-a-month payments are out of her league—for now.

Ultimately, Aimee was swayed in her decision by the industry's most power forces: personal relationships and quality after-sale service. Aimee still remembered the honesty and professionalism of the salesperson who sold her the used '92 she'd bought while still in college. That particular salesperson and the service department had really bent over backward to resolve a problem. So Aimee made a call. Then she drove an extra 15 miles to what was now called an Auto*Starr Center.

* * *

Meanwhile, using the voice-recognition technologies of their wall-panel PC-TV, Paul and Jan Daniels didn't even have to leave the comfort of their family room to configure, "test drive," order, finance, and arrange for delivery of their purchase.

Configuring their car online was a new—and frankly, exciting—experience. When buying cars in the past, the Daniels had been limited to choices such as the exterior color, a V-6 or V-8, and saying "yea" or "nay" to optional equipment. Also, getting the best deals on options generally required buying packages, and that usually meant getting some options they could live without, and forgoing some they might have liked instead.

What's more, like 95 percent of Americans, the Daniels had always bought their cars straight off the lot. So it had really been the dealers who'd ordered the cars, making educated guesses as to what customers wanted most.

But this was truly *their* car! Not only had the automaker put its offer online, it had allowed consumers to radically customize the product. The Daniels weren't simply choosing or rejecting *optional* equipment, they were also picking *major systems* from a range of suppliers. They'd visited the site two nights earlier and jointly pored over all the various specs and prices. So now they were merely putting it all together.

"The Dan-Lr XXL cockpit?" Paul asked, after pausing the program with a keystroke.

"Yup," his wife concurred.

"Red analog dials? Dual front buckets with the Safe-T Sensor response system . . . and the Jerry Garcia green fabric, right?" he continued.

"That's the deal," she said.

He spoke the appropriate commands, and the Internet program continued to talk the Daniels through the options—literally custom-building their car from the tires on up. Right before their eyes, their new car took shape! Pivoting on various axes, the virtual representation of their GL2000 was stunning. They could look at the exterior, pop the hood to examine the engine, and look inside to see various seat configurations.

When the Daniels were finished, the low hum of the engine filled the room and voice program asked:

"Would you like to test drive your car?"

Although they'd already driven a GL2000, this was a chance to see *their* car in action in highly realistic settings ranging from muddy backroads to the autobahn. The VR program gave a reasonable sense of how it accelerated, braked, and handled. Just for fun, they let Paul Jr. get a preview of how the world looked passing by from its back seat.

Next, with the aid of audio prompts and visual drop-down menus, Jan took care of the financing decisions. They were given a range of options, ranging from links to their own bank to paying cash via a proprietary virtual network set up to secure and ease such online transactions. They could also take advantage of the numerous alliances the carmaker had with various financial institutions.

They chose a 43-month payoff with a monthly inflation adjustment. Following that, the Daniels chose from a range of similarly innovative delivery options, each with differing costs, then waited 15 seconds until the order confirmation appeared. And they were finished.

Although they didn't realize it, the Daniels' specific order information was already spurring intense activity throughout a supply chain whose mantra was *connect everything*—and it was those connections that would put their vehicle in the Daniels' driveway within the next three days.

* * *

"Aimee, I'm glad you responded to my e-mail. Like I said, you're going to be amazed by how much things have changed around here," the salesperson, Pam Laughton, said shaking Aimee's hand.

"Just six months ago, our dealership became part to the Auto*Starr network," she continued. "It was either that, try to connect up with some other small independents, or go out of business. And it's been great."

"Whether you're buying from one of the Global Five or an independent, when you buy from Auto*Starr you get a commitment to service and support. We put our reputation behind the product. We put service into every produce we sell," Pam continued.

For one thing, she explained, Auto*Starr has the buying clout to give its customers better deals—and not just in the cars they sell. As one of the new network dealers, Auto*Starr focuses on the entire driving experience, and sells cars with "bundled" services. Through various alliances with brand-name companies in the energy, insurance, and other industries, Auto*Starr is the customer's one-stop source of some fairly substantial savings for everything from gasoline and tires to insurance and oil changes.

"Also, we take the hassles out of the buying process—with one price, no haggling," Pam said, as she escorted Aimee to her office—a room that looked nothing like the old, putty-colored holes-in-the-wall she recalled seeing at car dealers. Instead, it had a homey feel, complete with a couch and a large-screen display that would enable her to shop across various brands. When it came time to configure a car, Pam explained, she'd act as Aimee's personal advisor and help walk her through the process. Because Aimee was a previous customer and a member of the teachers' credit union, she'd qualify for a special discount.

Pam received no commission. Half of her compensation was a salary and the other half was goal-based, variable bonuses linked to Auto*Starr's corporate success, the profitability of this store, and personal goals such as customer satisfaction surveys and Auto*Starr's biannual testing of salespeople's product knowledge.

Down the hall were three, top-of-the-line VRTDs—virtual reality test drivers. Featuring a rig with a six-axis freedom-of-movement platform and 360-degree projection, their impressive verisimilitude was enhanced with surround sound speakers that even reproduced wind noise or the sound of passing cars on wet pavement. Each VRTD was loaded with the performance data of every major car that Auto*Starr sold, along with various road surface characteristics.

The result? Aimee could "test drive" a half dozen different models in an hour. "It's awesome. You get everything but the bugs hitting your windshield. Trust me, you'll love it!" Pam said enthusiastically. "You can really punch the pedals and sense how the car performs. Actually, it's a much truer test drive than the old deal of taking a spin around three or four blocks with the salesperson sitting in the back seat."

That was only one example of how Auto*Starr applied technology to enhance the buying experience and develop stronger customer connections. Knowledgeable salespeople were another differentiator. Several times a month all the salespeople acquired the latest product news via just-in-time, computer-based training.

Auto*Starr wanted to lock in customers for life, and was very blunt about it. As its found and CEO had said in a recent voice mail to all personnel: "Our mission isn't selling cars. It's meeting folks' transportation needs over their entire lifetimes. From that college grad buying a first new car . . . to a family man or woman . . . then a couple with kids . . . and finally, retired folks enjoying their golden years, we need to ask ourselves: How can we cater to those transportation needs? How do we keep the customer coming back to us?

This network dealer was, in fact, in a pitched battle with automakers for consumer loyalty. The multibillion-dollar question had become: Who owns the consumer? Mega-dealers such as Auto*Starr were counting on the answer being the, due to their reputation, policies such as no-questions-asked returns, and the convenience of their bundled services that came with every product. Lifetime, loyal consumers such as Aimee were drawn to Auto*Starr, where they could compare and select *across various automotive brands.*

"It's just like how my dad used to say he was going to Sears to buy tools, appliances, and TVs," Pam's general manager had once explained. "It was the retailer's good name that drew him in to buy with confidence. At Sears, he'd study what was on the shelves, look at the prices, get help from the sales folks, and choose whatever best met his needs."

Pam picked up a wireless remote, sat beside Aimee, and flicked on the large-screen display.

"Let's shop," she said.

The Marketing Executive

May 16, 2002—8:35 P.M.

When the Daniels placed their online order, the information was immediately distributed throughout the supply network to the assembler as well as all the tier-one suppliers. It also updated a database used by marketing executives to monitor sales. This database provided real-time answers to questions such as: What options and components are the hottest sellers, where, and with whom? How should our pricing be adjusted? What promotions are having the most impact? What upcoming innovations are consumers most frequently exploring online?

It was similar to the yield-management systems the airlines used. After all, a slot in an assembly line was just as perishable as a seat on an airplane.

Working on a wireless laptop in her hotel room, one of those executives, Carmen Sperli, was finalizing the marketing plan for the GL2000, 1.2.

It was a dream assignment, for three reasons.

First, the GL2000 was a truly innovative car that already rocked the auto world. This dramatically styled SUV boasted features such as self-cleaning glass on all four sides, drive-by-wire technologies, 100,000-mile warranty, new composite tires, and a hybrid engine with a regenerative braking system that got far better mileage than sedans of five years ago. The onboard computer system memorized each seat adjustment, wing- and rearview-mirror position, entertainment option, and steering wheel configuration to immediately and automatically customize itself to each driver.

Some of those features had been developed and tested in radically new ways. Speed to market took precedence, and products were expected to continue evolving after being launched. Here, they'd stolen a page from the computer industry by giving the marketplace several iterations of the product each year.

For instance, as Carmen understood it, the self-cleaning glass was coated with a layer of nonreflective material no more than a couple of atoms thick—a positively charged liquid that "flowed" slowly across the glass surface, to be continuously filtered and reapplied. This completely nonreflective glass was impressive—an offshoot of the special glass developed for use in some major museums' custom-made display cases. When Carmen had accidentally walked into a six-foot-wide pane of this Nu/Vu2 Glass at a trade show exhibit—and *still* couldn't see it—she immediately knew it would be a big part of their marketing campaign.

Carmen's plan included its own fair share of innovations. For one thing, she was forsaking some traditional advertising approaches in order to fund affinity marketing programs. These would provide links to airlines' frequent fliers clubs, major corporation, professional associations, and vacation sites such as Disneyland and Williamsburg, VA.

The affinity marketing programs would be win-win deals fostering two-way transfer of information—and business. The deal with Avis-Hertz had already proved the value of this approach when it helped to generate "buzz" about the car and gave the first six moths of sales a boost. So she was also proposing the offering of incentives to employees of select corporation that would link up with their existing corporate reward/benefits programs.

Another marketing innovation would be the "virtual reality test drives" of the GL2000. Traveling simulators would draw huge traffic at malls, auto shows, and golf courses.

Carmen's marketing plan used the Net and sophisticated information bases to identify and reach market niches. But here's what was really exciting: *the product would get smarter and better with use.* It would be an intelligent car. This was made possible by the sensor and computer capabilities of the GL2000 itself, what she referred to as its "iCar" capabilities.

"The GL2000 is not simply an automobile, it is an intelligent appliance," Carmen typed in the report. "The GL2000 has GPS, so we know where the consumer shops or goes for recreation, what routes he or she takes to work every day. It has a powerful CPU to store and process that information. And thanks to the satellite link, its advanced voice recognition technology, and pop-out or heads-up screens for passengers, it has the means to send and receive all sorts of data with *vast marketing significance.*"

Okay, that might be a bit of hyperbole, she thought to herself. But then again, was it?

"The GL2000 is like a credit card, which by itself is simply a piece of plastic," she continued to type. "But when *used,* it can provide a wealth of information that opens whole new worlds to marketers, both inside and outside of our industry."

Lately, Carmen had come to the conclusion that they were sitting on a cash cow, but nobody seemed to fully realize it! Every time they sold one of their products, they were getting back something of potentially even greater value—in-depth customer *information,* and the time of a captive audience of consumers that would be seated inside one of their products on a near-daily basis.

"We paid for that *information*—with a 10 percent discount information-release clause that the driver signed. We own that time. . . ." Carmen thought, her mind racing. "What would Bill Gates do with those two resources? Give them both away? Squander them? Set up his own network to sell advertising, information . . . services? But what services? How? With whom?"

For instance, would today's billboards go the way of Burma Shave signs? A GL2000 would "know," for instance, that a certain driver tended to visit a particular gas station when his tank was half empty. What if when the tank was a *third* empty, the driver received a discount offer to visit another station? The possibilities were endless. What a wonderful match of customized consumer information and captive audience!

Until now, everyone had focused only on how some aspects of the Internet would impact the automotive world. But Carmen had a vision that included the automobile as a viable portal to the Internet, thanks to improved voice-recognition technology and ever-more-hectic lifestyles. Why sit at home at night surfing the Net, when intelligent agents would bring you much of the news, entertainment, and information you sought each day—and present it in a pleasing interactive, audio format that demanded little effort on your part—while driving to and from work?

iCars would no longer be viewed as simply mechanical devices to get from Point A to Point B. They would be software-driven intelligent tools—in essence, time managers that allow drivers to maximize the value of the time spent in daily commutes and other travels.

That's where AUTO.cast came in. With this service, the GL2000 would download customized audio or video programs off the satellite network for the driver and/or the occupants. And all by voice command.

Driving to work, one person might listen to updates on her stocks, call down headlines from *The Wall Street Journal* and ask for more details, or possibly hear the first chapter of the new novel from a favorite author. Another might wish to hear classic country music, profiles on the college players just drafted by a favorite team, and PG-rated humor. All programming could be repeated, skipped, stored, or transmitted elsewhere in another format upon voice command. Naturally, the standard navigational and safety features would be part of the package. So would intelligent "shop bots." These voice-activated, intelligent agents were on-call 24 hours a day. When needed, they would search the Internet for particular products and services within specific parameters (such as prices, makes, characteristics) and work in concert with the GPS. So the driver could, for example, request "Please tell me how to get to the nearest gas station selling X-octane gas at a price lower than Y dollars, and nearest store selling product Z."

When buying a GL2000, the consumer would provide profile information—rich information to be mined—that would customize the news, entertainment, special features, search engines, foreign language programming access, radio streaming audio, and other components that were combined into this single package.

Carmen knew that her proposal to aggressively enter into this AUTO.cast consortium with several major media companies, including Disney and Time Warner, in time for version 1.3 had already caused a ruckus in her company's executive suites. Or so she'd been told. Carmen smiled.

Carmen also *knew* that once consumers experienced AUTO.cast, they'd be hooked on the carmaker's proprietary information and entertainment service. Many would become long-term loyal consumers—due to the service embedded in the product. But how to get them hooked? The answer seemed clear: They'd give the service away free for the first two years to anyone buying a GL2000.

She returned her thoughts back to the report at hand.

"The key question: Who 'owns' this information gathered through the portal of our automobiles? We propose that the Corporation aggressively stake ownership of it," she continued to write. "Others will also try to stake claim. Furthermore, the privacy battles in the courts and legislatures may rival anything we have experienced in the safety or environmental arena—but the outcomes are crucial to the long-term shareholder value of the Corporation."

She saved and logged off.

The Design Team

May 17, 2002—8:00 A.M.

Working at his company's Virtual Automotive Design Center in Silicon Valley, Jack Gordon was networked with colleagues worldwide. Jack, a native of Seattle, was the team's heavily recruited software/electronics guru, and still a bit bemused by the culture shock of dealing with all these displaced Detroiters. But since more than half of the design and engineering costs of a car were now in electronics, rather than stamped metal or extruded plastics, Jack had clout and he knew it.

His team's challenge: Develop the next-generation replacement for the four-year-old Millennium. They didn't have much time. The automotive industry had operated on six- or seven-year product life cycles. Now that was down to 24 months. And that cycle had to be cut in half. Jack was used to that environment. After all, PC companies operated in *three-month* new product development cycles.

To meet the engineering challenges, Jack's team was drawing on a range of approaches—including consumer research from the Net, and the use of math data and virtual models that enabled "no more clay" design. After all, if Boeing could build a plane without a full-scale prototype, why would they need one? Also, "drive before build" simulators provided a wealth of safety test data and allowed assessment of vehicle performance under various situations.

In fact, it was a year to the day that the company fired off its last crash-test dummy on a high-G sled. They'd outsourced all crash testing to a firm that used computer simulations. It made sense to outsource anything that wasn't a core competence. Today, victory didn't come to the carmaker with the most competencies—it went to the one best able to marshal inside or outside intellectual capital. And that's where Jack excelled. Let people and companies focus on what they did best, then apply that expertise to reach a higher goal than the other guy was shooting for.

Using this outside firm's crash simulator, for example, they could cost-effectively conduct hundreds or even thousands of various crash scenarios on the computer: Head-ons, side impacts, accidents on slick surfaces, collisions with heavier vehicles with bumpers of various heights, traveling at various speeds. Plus, thanks to the efforts of a team of forensic doctors commissioned by this outside firm, vastly improved virtual testing dummies had been engineered that provided accurate projections of sustained injuries—from minor skin contusions, to broken bones, to fatalities.

Some of the most valuable data came from the "black box" embedded in all of their cars. Onboard sensors would automatically collect crash-related data and send it to their crash site monitoring service. That data had also helped the contractor upgrade its crash test simulator.

Jack would start his morning by wearing his "chairperson" hat at a meeting of the crash safety task force. He was asking the team to begin working on a total safety platform, not for the next Millennium upgrade but for one that would be introduced two generations down the road in order to leapfrog the competition.

It was a mixed group—half of the people were from outside the Company. Jack liked it that way. The creative brainstorming and solutions that came out of these collaborative sessions got his blood flowing. After he walked in and slid a box of bagels onto the table, Jack nodded at Pete Ketzler from the firm that did all of their virtual crash testing. As he glanced around the room, Jack saw a new face. He seemed to recall being told this new guy had been working on transponders or something for the aerospace industry.

At the last meeting, Jack had hit them with a challenge, "Forget about a 100 percent survival rate in a 55-mph head-on," he'd said, tongue only partially in cheek. "I want to be able to set a cyber-egg on the lap of one of Pete's wire-frame cyber-dummies and, after smashing the Millennium at 55, to poach and eat that egg for breakfast."

Jack hit them with another challenge this morning.

"We need to change the paradigm again," he said, ignoring a couple of groans. "Up until now, we've been dealing with things from the moment of impact. But now I can mount a buck-ninety-eight sensor on each bumper and side of the car, link it to the CPU, and tell you that if this car is going 58 mph and is 80 feet from a solid object, it's about to have what you might call a 'catastrophic event.'

"Now, *you tell me*—what would you do with that information and that extra time? Give me your wish list guys. What systems would deploy? Does the frame change its characteristics? What happens to the brakes, steering, the torque delivered by the engine? Do the seats change pitch? Does the headrest move forward? Do the onboard air bags have enough time to fire off more gently? Does some sort of Kevlar-reinforced air bumper fire off outside the car? Does the dashboard . . ."

Someone spoke up, interrupting. "Not enough data. Tell me about the other car."

Everyone looked toward the end of the table. It was the new guy.

"Tell me the weight of the other car. How many occupants. Its exact speed. What safety devices are loaded on this model that will deploy? Is there a kid in the back seat? What will happen if it brakes one wheel to change the angle of impact by merely 15 degrees. What if I do the same in concert?"

"Uh-huh? And who is gonna tell my car all of that?" Jack asked.

"The other car will," he replied.

The room was silent.

Then Peter Ketzler spoke up. "And then that's where all of the gazillion gigabytes of virtual crash test information we've downloaded to you folks from our crash simulator over the past six months really come into play. Different scenarios, different responses. No driver can react as fast—or as intelligently. No single car can solve a head-on scenario alone. And this will make Jack's bosses grin from ear to ear, because the system can be downloaded and installed on the 2006 Millennium upgrade, you guys get to build the new industry platform that everyone else will have to build off."

"Okay, good. Let's explore some possibilities," Jack said, tossing a bagel to the new guy.

The Engineering Team

May 17, 2002—8:35 P.M. (New Delhi Time)

Darshna was finally logging off in New Delhi—and leaving a "hello, and good morning" video message to Kevin, a fellow engineer starting his workday in the U.S.

Kevin was seated at a powerful, connected 3-D color workstation—part of the global "cockpit" team for the Millennium replacement.

Although he was technically on the payroll of the tier-one systems supplier charged with designing, engineering, manufacturing, and delivering that cockpit, Kevin was co-located at the carmaker's facility. What's more, the guy in the cubicle next door was from the *tier-two* supplier of the arm test and side panels.

Collaboration was the name of the game. Systems and people were integrated to make a true team—everyone was connected, regardless of geography or corporate affiliation.

Knowledge sharing was also a big part of Kevin's day-to-day life as a "connected designer." Just three or four years ago, Kevin would devote more than a day out of each week simply *looking* for existing knowledge. Now, powerful search engines provided answers. And networks collected, organized, and distributed everyone's knowledge, so that no one was literally reinventing the other guy's wheel.

Relationships were vastly changed, too. For example, that tier-two guy next door sure sucked up shamelessly to him as the systems supplier . . . the way Kevin used to court the carmaker's chief engineers.

The design/engineering teams were facing some tough challenges. For example, the edict had come down—this car shall be a true global product. Standardized platforms are a must. Right-left steering wheel configurations must be engineered in. It must be a "green" car—exceeding both European requirements for recyclability as well as those Congress just passed.

Another key challenge: It must be thoroughly upgradeable. For example, interchangeable body panels and interior components must allow the consumer to radically reconfigure and "refresh" the car's outer design and inside look. The onboard computer must be able to download upgraded software via the satellite or built-in cell phone to improve engineer performance and suspension handling.

Kevin laughed at the video mailgram he saw in the corner of his work station screen: "Hey, Kev. No need to run a test of the APV component—we've already done so and I've downloaded the data to the respository. By the way, Jack already hit all of us on this side of the planet with today's safety challenge. Think poached eggs. Cheers, Darsh."

The Connected Value Web

May 17, 2002—10:00 A.M.

Jon Peterson was one of 20 systems suppliers taking part in this Friday morning videoconference with the assistant plant manager of the contract manufacturer charged with assembling the GL2000.

It's a biweekly event. These teleconferences allow the companies that used to be called OEMs—or in this case, a contract manufacturer—to discuss production requirements, review the assembly schedule, and interact with each supplier. The assistant plant manager was sitting in his office with 20 video display images on the wall, allowing him to survey the entire team.

"Can everybody meet this schedule? Is anyone experiencing problems? Will orders for dual-fuel powerplants or Ultrasuede seats stress capacity?" he asked.

These meetings, along with real-time testing and Web-based simulation, identified any potential bottlenecks in the supply chain based on up-to-date order information.

Under real-time order management, the online order submitted from the Daniels went straight to Jon's computers at the same time that it also hit the OEM and all the other suppliers in the Bill of Materials using collaborative forecasting products. This was a "push" planning system—the order was pushed out to the supplier. The actual release and shipping of material to the assembler was then "pulled" from the suppliers through an electronic kanban based on actual usage at the assembly plant. This innovative push/pull manufacturing was implemented throughout the value network.

From his perspective as a supplier, Jon knew success rested on the ability to integrate his business with his customer as part of a synchronized supply chain, and to deliver small lot quantities that moved with greater frequency. OEMs used to seek 20 turns a year, keeping two weeks' inventory on hand. Now they were doing 100-plus turns annually. But even that two-day inventory had been deemed far too high—and that worried him.

The driving force for this greater supply chain responsiveness was consumers such as the Daniels family—who not only ordered a highly customized product via the Internet, but had just gone back online to *change* the color of their instrumentation from red to green.

The contract manufacturer operated under the Dell model. That is, it didn't tie up any money in inventory. In fact, it had achieved *negative* working capital by not beginning work on a car until payment had been received, and by delaying its own payments to suppliers.

So it was no big surprise when the assistant plant manager concluded the videoconference by announcing a big change in its supplier payment policies. Previously, they'd paid only at the time the vehicle sold. Now he hears Henri say that they're borrowing another page from Dell; payment will be made seven days *after* the vehicle sells.

"The more things change, the more they stay the same," Jon thought to himself.

The Assembly Line

May 17, 2002—1:00 P.M.

Following that Friday morning videoconference, Assistant Plant Manager Henri Crozet left his office to give a tour of the new assembly plant to a local business reporter. That was an important part of Henri's job. Government and community connections were critical.

The assembly line was a clean plant in a renovated building. And the reporter was hearing how this former aerospace firm, frozen out of the last round of mergers, had found a new lease on life as a niche assembler of automobiles.

"OEMs are looking to downsize their capital investments. They see what's happening on Wall Street," Henri said, talking loudly, as he took the reporter on the nickel tour of the facility. "Companies with intangible assets are valued higher than those saddled with the 'bricks and mortar.' That's where we come in. We have what they need to outsource their assembly process: the skilled people, the outstanding process controls, the quality culture . . . and yes, some bricks and mortar."

Henri grew serious. "A few years ago, it would have been considered insane to even suggest that an OEM would outsource its entire assembly function. But outsourcing actually has been going on for a long time. Go back to the days of Henry Ford. Back then Ford did everything from manufacturing to marketing, to the extent that he offloaded sand and ore to make his own steel. In the 1990s, the OEMs really stepped up their outsourcing of the design and engineering of systems to suppliers. Now we're seeing assembly being outsourced—and it makes sense.

"After all, what's the OEM's only real goal?" he asked, as they walked along an overhead catwalk that ran the length of the bustling assembly line. Answering his own question, he stated: "It's to get a great product out into the marketplace with its nameplate on it so that the profits flow back through it. Within the next five years, I believe you'll see some of the OEMs completely outsource all their assembly and stick to design and marketing. Conversely, others—including some Japanese firms with U.S. facilities—will focus solely on assembly as what *they* do best . . . and they'll be our competitors."

They walked down a metal stairway onto the floor.

"No two GL2000s are the same—they're totally customized. Flexible and adaptive manufacturing techniques are critical to our success," Henri pointed out as they walked down the line. "So is speed. Paying that much for a hot, customized product via the Internet—people expect to see it in their driveways within three days."

Henri walked the reporter over to where a red instrument panel was being yanked out and replaced with a green one. "Last-minute change order must have come in. We can do it, and still meet the ship date," he explained. "If it was a major, last-minute change that bollixed up our planning and sequencing, they'd give the customer a choice—pay a $350 surcharge to take delivery one time, or give us an extra day. Personally, I would have kept the red instruments and lost that God-awful designer interior—yeeech!"

They walked further upstream in the assembly line.

"We've had to change the entire manufacturing paradigm," Henri continued. "For decades cars have been produced through three fundamental steps. You *stamp* metal. You *weld* it to connect the major pieces. Then you *paint* it. The problem with that stamp-weld-paint model is that it requires a massive infrastructure. A traditional assembly line starts at about $800 million. This assembly plant right here could have been built from the ground up for a tenth of that cost—about $80 million.

"Traditional auto manufacturing models caused two major problems for the OEMs," he continued. "First of all, you really can't put one in a lot of developing countries because of the cost and requirements for supporting infrastructure. Second, it's cost-prohibitive to switch over to new technologies. Right now, a plant using traditional assembly techniques has to stay in place 10 to 15 years to pay for itself.

"But look at Silicon Valley manufacturing sites. They're completely retooled every two to three years. You can't do that with billion-dollar plants. You need to be able to design your manufacturing changeover along with your product life-cycle changeover."

The reported asked: "So what are you doing in place of the old stamp-weld-paint model?"

"Poured titanium frame with a carbon-reinforced polymer outer shell," Henri replied. "But we're not married to it. There are plenty of other options. That's merely what we're using now."

Henri pointed out other features, such as the fact that all equipment was mounted on wheels and rollers, allowing for faster changeovers. As the reporter watched, a truck with a Federal Express logo on its side pulled up to one of several doors positioned along the length of the assembly line and, with the aid of remotely controlled robotic arms, unloaded only the customized cockpit interiors needed for the next two hours—in the precise sequence the orders had been arranged to come down the line.

"We've outsourced all supply chain transportation to Fed Ex—from the raw materials to delivery of the finished car. Let me show you how we sequence," Henri said. He tried to introduce the reporter to Ellis, the plant's sequencing guru, who was on a speak phone call.

A supplier was saying: "Yes, I can do it. But you have to take 10 four-doors out of the schedule and move them to Sunday. I can get the extra doors to you on Sunday. If I have to get them to you on Saturday, I gotta run my line with 10 hours of OT, and that's gonna dump my cost structure in the. . . ."

"We'll catch him later," Henri told the reporter. "But to sum up, it's no longer just Ford versus Toyota, or whatever. Value networks—what we used to call supply chains—are competing against each other. This is where it all comes together. And it's dangerous or fatal for anyone in *our network* to get complacent."

The reporter asked, "What's this I hear about you entering an alliance to help Auto*Starr introduce its own private-label automobile?"

"Off the record?" Henri asked, taken aback slightly by the question.

The reporter nodded.

"We're not there yet. But it's going to happen. And we intend to be their partners when it does."

Speaking off the record, Henri confirmed what the reporter already knew—that the network dealer Auto*Starr planned to market its own customizable pick-up trucks.

"I call this project the Jenny-mobile, myself," Henri laughed, "because it's how my little daughter connects those plastic clip-together building blocks. You know—a piece from here, a piece from there."

He explained that, along with outsourcing, the industry was being reshaped by another trend—standardization. "Suppliers are standardizing components and systems, much as the PC and electronics industry in general did a long time ago. Ask yourself: Why can all the PC-makers put together their boxes from the same parts and offer improved performance and value year after year? Because, for one thing, they're highly standardized. Everyone complies with common price structures and electrical specs. So if a manufacturer wants to replace one hard drive with another, no problem. Same thing if you want to plug a new sound card into your computer.

"In the late 1990s suppliers began to build and ship entire systems—such as rolling chassis or interiors," Henri pointed out. "That made the OEMs *systems integrators*. Right now, they are letting customers customize the product—but only within their prescribed family of systems.

"In the future, Auto*Starr is talking about taking it to the next logical step—allowing the customer to be the ultimate systems integrator with systems from various OEMs and tier-one suppliers. If standardization continues, soon we'll be able to buy major systems and put them together in a whole range of configurations. Wild, huh?" said Henri.

"You won't be limited to the design stylings of the OEMs either. I'm told that Auto*Starr is contacting some of the top-notch design houses to create fresh looks that can be bolted on existing chassis. And frankly, they've done some good work—I saw one of Oscar De La Puerto's sketches. For a guy who designs purses and eyeglasses, it was pretty sharp!"

"When that happens, you'll be seeing some of the systems suppliers and design houses advertising their products direct to consumers. Do you remember the 'Intel inside' ad campaign?" Henri asked.

The reporter looked puzzled.

"Too young, I guess," Henri said. "The point is, what you've just seen here is only the beginning. Consumer demand for greater customization will help push it along. Remember, a car is most families' second greatest investment, after a house. And who wants to live in Levittown anymore?"

"Can we go back on the record?" the reporter asked, her interest clearly piqued by this vision of the future.

"Sure," Henri replied. "Come on. I want you to meet our HR liaison. He'll tell you what we're doing with our compensation and education program."

The Delivery

May 18, 2002—3:45 P.M.

Since the distribution of the GL2000 had been outsourced to Fed Ex, order-to-delivery time had been cut to three days. In itself, that was a major boost to the industry, which used to have 60 days of finished-goods inventory sitting on factory and dealer lots. That was $50 billion of working capital squandered—now it was being put to better use.

When the Daniels ordered their GL2000 online, they had a range of delivery options. For example, they had toyed with the idea of saving a few bucks by picking it up at the local Wal-Mart. In another win-win deal, the carmaker had an arrangement with that ubiquitous retailer to utilize its vast parking lots. When a customer arrived to pick up a new car, he or she simply provided the delivery code number and a driver's license to be scanned. While waiting for confirmation, the customer was offered a hot dog, a Coke, and a $10 Wal-Mart coupon for automotive accessories. That delivery option would have lowered the Daniels' distribution charge from $600 to $300. If they had wanted to save $500, they could have driven straight to the plant to pick up their new GL2000.

But Jan had just received a promotion, and they'll be moving, so time was short—the Daniels had their car delivered straight to their driveway for an extra $79.

Aimee, on the other hand, showed up at Auto*Starr to pick up the 2004 Millennium that she was able to get at a discount. It was an emotional experience for her—one she shared with the salesperson, Pam.

Not surpisingly, there was a rose on the front seat with a personalized note from the company's CEO when Aimee picked up the car. There was also a complimentary Auto*Starr Discount Coupon Book, offering deals at restaurants, movies, airlines, and other establishments.

But Pam had even more good news that would make Aimee a loyal customer for life. Auto*Starr has just undertaken a program that will provide her with free service for the next three years.

(Auto*Starr knows that, with warranty coverage, this will only cost a couple of hundred dollars a year at most, whereas value exchange analysis shows that a loyal customer such as Aimee equals $1,000 profit every three years.)

For Paul and Jan Daniels, much of the emotion comes from the car itself. With the GL2000, Dan finally feels downright excited behind the wheel, or in this case, behind a joystick of a drive-by-wire car that is already learning and recording his driving mannerisms in order to boost its performance. Maybe a bit too excited. He's been speeding. The flashing lights of the squad car pull him over, and bring him back down to earth. The officer, holding a palm-sized device, appears at the crystal-clear window.

"Sir, do I have your permission to download the last two minutes of your vehicle's performance data?" he inquires. Thanks to recent probable-cause, search-and-seizure rulings by the Supreme Court, the policeman has to specify the parameters of the data download. Nowadays, the criminal's own car often makes the best witness as to his whereabouts.

Meanwhile, over at the nearest GL2000 dealer, the sales manager faces another challenge: How do we stay connected to the Daniels? Not only haven't they dealt face to face with anyone during the entire buying experience, they are moving to Tampa.

Technology will help enable these connections, too. For one thing, when the GL2000's odometer senses the vehicle is approaching its 15,000-mile service checkup, a message will appear on its display from the local Tampa dealers' consolidated service center. And if built-in sensors report that the batteries or other systems aren't performing properly, it will let the Daniels schedule a service appointment right then and there via the console keypad.

The dealer will also use its own technologies to further the customer connections. For instance, the dealership will transfer news of the Daniels' move to the local Tampa bank with which they have an alliance, as well as transfer all of Dan's service records for his other cars and purchases to their local Tampa affiliate dealer.

A touch of his index finger fires up the modem on his PC, and the sales manager hears the connections being made.

CONCLUSION

As these brief scenarios illustrate, tomorrow is likely to be both very different and similar to today. Just like the science fiction of the past, some of the predicted startling changes will occur, some will not. Some of our lives will be surprisingly unchanged and other unforeseen changes will sweep through our world.

Some events are already unfolding.

At the start of 1999, for example, the Internet began to fundamentally reshape the automotive industry's structure, operations, and relationships. A franchise dealer, Saab of Santa Ana, California, announced that it would launch an Internet Web site that would allow consumers to:

- Shop available inventory.
- Arrange for test drives.
- Handle financing.

- Make the purchase.
- Arrange for delivery.

The CEO of Saab Cars USA said he expected Internet sales to eventually account for 30 percent of Saab sales.

South Korean automaker Daewoo took e-commerce a step further. It announced plans to start selling cars directly to consumers by way of an Internet site that bypasses the dealer entirely. Car-buyers will also be able to capitalize on deals Daewoo has made with financing and insurance partners.

In March, General Motors introduced its Internet-based car-selling service, GM BuyPower, which lets consumers review the inventory of local dealers as well as get current rebate deals and price quotes. GM expects about three-quarters of its dealers to be linked to the service. Ford's Buy-Connection and DaimlerChrysler's web site, GetaQuote, also allow car shoppers to get quotes from their dealers.

These sites—which link consumers, OEMs, and dealers—are important, first steps by the industry. However, there is a key piece missing from the puzzle: suppliers must also be connected to other players via the Internet. The radical changes explored in this book can only occur if all parties are able to effectively exchange real-time information—and engage in joint planning, scheduling, and problem solving—as participants in a completely integrated, well-synchronized value network.

Computers and Communications

It is also safe to say that technology will continue to provide new solutions to old problems and new challenges. Computers will continue to become even faster, more powerful, and hold more information. Communications will become more pervasive, easier, and less expensive. Technology-enabled processes will reduce time and distance to absolute minimums.

Speed and connectivity will be in lockstep. Projects or jobs, whether designing or buying a new car or truck, will occur faster than ever with no wasted energy. The dead time between tasks (queue time) will disappear. All the padding will be stripped from planning and scheduling. As processes become superefficient, barriers between organizations and functional areas will become almost totally blurred. Better design will be needed to prevent breakdowns that were previously masked by the nonproductive dead times.

The Value of Intangibles

A third key concept—the value of intangibles—was also on the minds of automotive executives at the start of 1999. Many industry executives found themselves seeking reasons for companies' moribund Wall Street performance. At the same time, various Internet stocks continued to soar—some believed to unreasonable heights—more on the basis of their *promise* than as a reflection of their performance.

But the automotive industry continues to hold tremendous promise. Entering a new century, the industry is poised to bring incredible innovations to a global market. In fact, the automotive industry has a wealth of the intangibles that are most valued in a connected economy—such as its outstanding people, knowledge, well-developed brands, and relationships. The ability to leverage the power of all those intangibles will be important differentiators among automotive companies.

Fast Forward

Will the iCar function exactly as we described it? Is the "push/pull" system of planning and order filling the future of manufacturing? Will totally customizable "Jenny-mobiles" give consumers even more choices than they have today?

Will auto retailers evolve into *transportation consultants*—offering a complete range of integrated, innovative products and services? How will these changes in the automotive industry affect society, from the environmental impacts to privacy debates and law enforcement?

Only time will tell. And it will be an exciting time for anyone connected to the automotive industry.

Automotive suppliers and manufacturers have unparalleled opportunities to leapfrog competitors with new innovations. Likewise, the dealers that reinvent themselves and deliver new levels of value will fight for customer mindshare. And the big winner in today's connected economy is the automotive consumer—empowered with more information and more choices than ever before.

Technology will always be an important force for change. But in the new century, it's the people-related elements that will grow the most in value. People cement the sale, conceive the design, solidify the engineering, create the marketing, and maintain the relationship year after year. The world is moving from transactions to relationships, from individuals to teams, from generic products to loyalty-based brands.

Some elements of life will not change. Cars will still be an emotional purchase for most people, the second largest purchase after a home (or third, if you count the various financial products being purchased to fund retirements).

Automobiles will not be replaced by mass transit. We will go to work, to school, to play by car; we will go to shop and to fish by car; just as we always have. But the emergence of the iCar means we will also work and learn and play and shop in our cars and trucks. We will create and use and gather information for ourselves and others in our cars.

The iCar will not be simply an upgraded version of today's models with a few unconnected gizmos added. It will have the intelligence and awareness to help us deal with the major issues that matter most—such as sensing an impending crash and networking with other vehicles to collaboratively solve a problem and save lives. And it will help with the small details woven into our lives, whether it's a business person looking for a good seafood restaurant in a strange town or a parent using a voice-activated online service to pull down the audio home page of the local school district to check the lunch menu while driving the kids to school.

Our cars will still be portals to our lives—taking us to familiar places, but also bringing us to exciting new points of destination.

Appendix B

Automotive News PACE™ Award Recipients, 1998–1999

Companies that welcome and foster change—and view innovation as a process, not an end result—prosper through a continuous flow of innovations. The Automotive News PACE™ Awards, jointly presented by Ernst & Young LLP and Automotive News, explore this ongoing innovation process within the automotive supply industry. PACE examines how today's leading suppliers give birth to innovative products and services. The goal is to identify, analyze, and honor innovators—and to learn from them in the process.

The detailed judging process to select the annual PACE finalists and honorable mentions examines applicant companies along three dimensions: leadership, uniqueness, and results.

This appendix describes the innovations of PACE Award recipients of 1998 and 1999—the "best of the best."

1999

ASHA CORPORATION
Santa Barbara, California

For its GERODISC™ limited-slip, hydromechanical coupling device.

GERODISC, ASHA Corporation's limited-slip, hydromechanical coupling device, sends torque to the wheel or wheels of a vehicle with the most traction, thereby eliminating wheel slip. The coupling transfers torque between the left and right wheels of a FWD vehicle and, if there is a GERODISC in the transfer case, between the front axle and the rear axle of a four-wheel and/or AWD vehicle. The technology is a simple solution to a complex automotive problem: distribution of front wheel drive capacity. The device utilizes speed differential of the wheels to generate hydraulic pressure that activates mechanical wear plates, which transfer torque instantaneously, without driver input, in a continuously variable manner, as needed. It functions invisibly to the driver and provides major improvements in traction and handling characteristics.

The device replaces more expensive, complex, heavier systems and provides breakthrough performance in virtually all drive systems. It is estimated that the device can save OEMs 55 pounds and $75 per vehicle over alternative systems, with even larger potential savings due to elimination of current FWD architecture. The device can function as a stand-alone traction control and stability device or be integrated with current and future electronic systems.

The technology has been licensed to several Tier One suppliers and is commercially available on the 1999 Jeep Grand Cherokee under the DaimlerChrysler name Vari-Lok™

in its Quadra Drive™ system. The vehicle won "4 × 4 Vehicle of the Year," and the system is now regarded as the benchmark in the four-wheel drive segment. GERODISC will be introduced on several vehicles under various names in the next few years, and is "changing the rules of the game" in drivetrain technology.

The 1999 PACE Award is given to ASHA for its strategic vision in applying technology in an innovative way—against the trend to increased electronic controls—to produce a device that significantly improves vehicle safety and handling.

BENTELER AUTOMOTIVE CORPORATION
Grand Rapids, Michigan

For its WIN88 Rear Twist Beam Axle for the 1998 Ford Windstar.

Benteler, a 1998 PACE Award winner, knew it had to innovate to capture the Ford Windstar 98 rear-axle order from another long-standing supplier. Benteler creatively drew on its history of tubular products processes and manufacturing to apply them to what was for Benteler a new and different automotive product. By replacing the long-standard stamped U-shape crossbeam and torsion bar with a single crushed tube, Benteler significantly lowered cost to the customer, reduced weight by 9 percent, and improved the resulting product with increased stiffness and increased intrinsic quality by eliminating parts and welds.

Key enabling innovations came from workers ranging from engineers to a toolmaker on the shop floor, reflecting Benteler's continuing success in fostering innovation throughout its organization. In the process, Benteler actually improved on a different design on the basis of which it initially won the Windstar contract.

In addition, Benteler faced a last-minute engineering challenge to eliminate a warranty problem in the existing design due to excessive bending of the trailing arm. Forced once again to innovate, Benteler worked with a key outside supplier to develop a unique zone heat-treating process for flat stampings. This required finding and learning to stamp a suitable heat-treatable alloy. The company is already applying this innovation to a new design for bumpers, allowing Benteler to develop and market a product line in which it had no prior experience. In developing this product, Benteler has tapped resources, both external and internal, and designed proprietary equipment and processes to build a patented product. In addition, Benteler's success with the original Windstar program has helped it to win the contracts for the rear-axle assembly for the Ford Escort replacement in both Europe and North America, and the front chassis/engine mount for the Chrysler Neon replacement.

DELPHI AUTOMOTIVE SYSTEMS

Delphi Saginaw Steering Systems
Saginaw, Michigan

For its E-Steer™ electronic steering system.

Delphi Saginaw Steering Systems is successfully commercializing a full-performance, total steering system that is driven electronically, using brushless motors to provide the power assist. By eliminating all hydraulics and using an electric motor for the power assist, E-Steer provides a number of innovative benefits: relatively easy tuning of all steering characteristics, even at the consumer level; variability in the design of power steering packages and their configuration and performance; "engine off" steering assist capability, since the system uses the vehicle's battery as its power source; fuel consumption savings; and the elimination of hydraulic fluids, seals, pumps, and hoses, meaning simplified manufacturing, weight savings, and environmental benefits.

E-Steer has now gone beyond prototype concepts and steering-assist systems. It is being commercialized in Europe on the Opel Gamma S 4300, the VW 119, and the Fiat 188. In North America it has been selected for the new GM delta platform, on which Sunfire and Cavalier cars will be built. These applications will total about two million units.

This innovation has been enabled by unrestricted engineering vision and by continuing creative uses of brushless motors and microchip and software capabilities and designs. The initial E-Steer system is positioned to lead to new opportunities in the future for Delphi-S, including potential eventual use with collision-avoidance and drive-by-wire systems of the future.

THE GOODYEAR TIRE & RUBBER COMPANY
Akron, Ohio

For its "Run Flat" Eagle Fl GS EMT tire technology.

Goodyear has developed passenger car run-flat tire technology to the point that it is now commercially viable to eliminate the spare tire, jack, and extra wheel in a new car, providing numerous safety, security, and weight and space-saving advantages to the manufacturer and to consumers, without the need for special wheels. New Chevrolet Corvette and Plymouth Prowler models are so equipped.

The Goodyear Eagle Fl GS EMT is uniquely capable of being fitted on standard, conventional wheels and is rated to run up to 200 miles at 55 mph, with zero inflation pressure. Vehicle handling and maneuvering characteristics are virtually unchanged in the run-flat condition. Run-Flat-equipped vehicles also include low-pressure warning systems visible to the driver.

The technology, in principle, is simple—specially formulated and controlled rubber reinforced sidewalls strengthened to permit an unchanged tire profile without air inflation. Depending on applications and desired run characteristics, the sidewall content can be varied, allowing a range of performance levels.

The safety, security, and convenience of not being immobilized along the roadway is a significant consumer advantage that is consistent with the innovation implicit in the PACE Award. This technology reinforces Goodyear's image as an innovation leader that develops new products in anticipation of manufacturers' and consumers' needs and desires.

With the increased interest in safety, convenience, cargo space, weight savings, and energy conservation, Goodyear is committed to extending applications to other models for aftermarket fitting and further uses of the technology.

MERITOR AUTOMOTIVE, INC.

Troy, Michigan

For its RHP Highway Parallelogram Trailer Air Suspension System, with integrated slider, trailer axles, and brakes.

Meritor's RHP Highway Parallelogram Air Suspension System has changed the basis of competition in this rapidly growing segment of the trailer suspension industry. Meritor's innovation, compact and lightweight suspension system, utilizes a revolutionary design that eliminates the traditional trailing-arm suspension and replaces it with a tandem suspension system, producing a parallel movement of the trailer's air springs. This, in turn, allows for the integration of a more efficient slider and single unified frame bracket, which, with Meritor's other existing undercarriage components, such as axles and brakes, can now be configured and delivered to the customer as a complete "bolt-on suspension system." The current industry practice generally requires final assembly of each air suspension system ordered.

Meritor's innovative system also results in dramatic safety and handling improvements. These include the elimination of "dock walk" while the trailer is being loaded or unloaded by forklift, under improved safety conditions, as well as the elimination of back slap, axle roll torque, and diving and hopping while braking when the trailer is being operated on the road. The improved handling and control characteristics result in significantly improved driver safety and comfort, as well as reduced wear and stress on the equipment.

The new design is also easier to service, reducing operating, maintenance, and repair costs. Its reduction in overall weight also lowers daily operating fuel costs and increases equipment flexibility, permitting greater loads and lowering back-haul costs.

Working closely with major truck OEMs, Meritor has gained rapid market acceptance for its new suspension system and has created a unique and commercially beneficial product for its customers.

MOTOROLA SEMICONDUCTOR PRODUCTS SECTOR
Austin, Texas

For its MPC555 PowerPC microcontroller, with embedded flash memory.

Motorola's Semiconductor Products Sector has designed a new, powerful, highly integrated, controller chip, the MPC555, for power train control in automobiles, addressing future needs in performance, fuel efficiency, and emissions. It is indeed innovative and commercial, and changes the rules of the game. Expectations of functionality in engine controllers will change as a result of this innovation. Because of its flash memory, the MPC555 can support engine types from 4 to 12 cylinders, in gasoline, diesel, or hybrid vehicles. Software unique to engine type can be installed after the controller is mounted in the vehicle. Additionally, the flash memory means reduction in number of controllers needed for multiple vehicle types, reduced time to market, flexibility in recalling or upgrading engine control characteristics, and reprogramming at the dealer level.

Previously, software that runs engine control systems resided in read-only memory (ROM); this device permits subsequent installation of new options, and is still cost-competitive. In addition, the MPC555's flash memory enables it to operate at temperatures up to 125° C, so it may be used in harsh, automotive applications and environments—inside an engine compartment or transmission, for example, where it need not take up real estate in a dedicated housing.

The MPC555 provides Motorola and its customers with one standard product usable in a wide variety of vehicles and circumstances, thus avoiding the complexity of manufacturing, inventory, and delivery problems that come with production of a large number of custom devices for many different customers.

The new controller has met all the demands of its early commercial adopters, while setting new price-performance standards.

STACKPOLE, LIMITED
Oakville, Ontario, Canada

For extending the capabilities of powdered metal parts.

Stackpole has created high-load-bearing powdered metal parts, with a more complex geometry than can be economically machined from conventional forgings, at a cost savings of 30 to 40 percent. This innovation enlarges the envelope for complex mechanical component design at costs comparable to those of simple geometry parts.

An example of such a part is the Gemini sprocket now used on GM 4T65 and 4T40 front-wheel-drive transmissions. The phased-tooth design is pressed in a unique split die, and the load-bearing surfaces are hardened with Stackpole's SelectDens™ process. The phased-tooth design reduces transmission noise, while eliminating the use of an extra sleeve bearing. Without the new Stackpole powdered metallurgy processes, such a design would be feasible only at a high premium cost.

This innovation included several process stages, beginning with customized powder formulation. The Stackpole SelectDens process promises not only to make powdered metal parts cost-competitive with existing heat-treated, low-alloy steel components, but to improve cost and performance of the subassemblies in which they are used through more imaginative overall design.

SelectDens and other process innovations have resulted from an ongoing 15-year program in powdered metal R&D, a competence in which Stackpole intends to remain a leader. It is enthusiastically developing further innovations in powdered metallurgy, and its award-winning technology should enable its customers to create award-winning designs for some time to come.

TELEFLEX, INC.

Teleflex Automotive Group
Troy, Michigan

For its adjustable pedal system for motor vehicles.

Teleflex stands out as a place where creativity is permanently on the executive agenda and where that emphasis has transformed the company from an old-line cablemaker to a cutting-edge developer of automotive technology. One such innovation is the patented adjustable pedal system that allows drivers of shorter stature to move the accelerator, brake, and clutch pedals closer while maintaining normal or desired seating position and optimum body positioning, and without altering pedal deployment action or angle. This permits safer air-bag deployment, safety restraint system effectiveness, and steering-wheel and instrument-panel-control access, while enhancing comfort, especially on long drives.

While the basic pedal system was acquired in the strategic purchase of Comcorp in 1997 by Teleflex, the principal inventors subsequently developed the device further, creating significant refinements that streamlined the system and resulted in a number of patents. The system was adopted as standard equipment on the 1999 Lincoln Navigator and as optional equipment on other models. With demand surpassing 260,000 units by the end of 1999, the adjustable pedal mechanism has been well received for its innovative safety, comfort, and convenience benefits.

The adjustable pedal mechanism serves as a cornerstone in Teleflex's own transformation as a company. With 70 to 80 patents won annually in recent years, Teleflex is positioned to build on its adjustable pedal technology with more new products in the near future. Its strategic alliances with organizations such as the Jet Propulsion Laboratory and NASA help keep Teleflex in a good innovative posture, a model for automotive industry innovation.

1998

GENTEX CORPORATION

First aspheric auto-dimming exterior mirror.

Gentex stands outs for its sharp strategic vision combined with high-tech innovative capabilities. A PACE Award winner in 1995 and 1997, the judges recognize Gentex this year for its aspheric auto-dimming exterior mirrors developed for use on Mercedes-Benz vehicles in Europe.

Although manufacturing aspheric auto-dimming mirrors drew upon existing electrochromic gel technologies, it also required a series of innovations to allow Gentex to mate two pieces of asymmetric glass at tolerances under .01 inches. Gentex faced challenging initial yields in January 1997, but its customer, Mercedes-Benz, raised production levels further by September. Gentex met these and other challenges, working with its suppliers to devise new molding techniques, developing sophisticated new in-house optical capabilities, and improving process yields.

Also impressive is the clarity of Gentex's strategic vision, which reflects its substantial, focused R&D commitments. Gentex now can supply auto-dimming units for all passenger-car rearview mirror applications, whether interior or exterior, flat, convex, or aspheric. It has increased product complexity while steadily reducing prices and deterred entry while expanding its overall market. Gentex has adhered to its mission of being the best at making mirrors, and has turned the 30-odd manufacturers of mirror modules from potential rivals into potential customers. It is even working to speed the regulatory acceptance of aspheric mirrors in the U.S.

DÜRR INDUSTRIES, INC.

Radiant floor construction (RFC) paint oven, which cures automotive coatings applied to dissimilar components or materials on the car body.

Dürr has demonstrated why it is an automotive business leader. Already the global leader in paint systems for automotive assembly plants with approximately 80 percent of the market, Dürr has come up with a revolutionary oven design that brings new competitive benefits to the company and its customers.

The fundamental change in the oven design is the use of the floor of the oven as the main heat source. The direct-fired air is forced through the Dürr-designed chamber in the floor to provide controlled radiant heat. Thus, without the need for a heat exchanger, products of combustion are excluded from the oven atmosphere. Air movement is kept to a minimum because of the use of radiant heat. Dürr has found that these factors have had a significant impact on reducing a big problem in paint shops: dirt and contamination associated with circulating air.

Dürr and its customers claim significant savings of up to 10 percent in the purchase and installation of the RFC oven, due in part to its modular design and the elimination of heat exchangers. In addition, it is estimated that operating savings will be significant in terms of costs of gas, electricity and filters saved over conventional designs.

Finally, and perhaps most important with Dürr's framework of innovation, this oven design yields more uniform curing rates on a variety of different substrates, thus allowing heavy metal, light metal, aluminum, and various plastics to be cured together in a single, simultaneous operation. The RFC oven solves previous problems and brings new customer benefits.

WAGNER LIGHTING DIVISION COOPER AUTOMOTIVE

Dodge Dakota and Durango front lamp assembly and related manufacturing and assembly processes.

Headlamp assemblies would appear to constitute a "mature" product and assembly opportunity. Yet the Wagner Lighting division of Cooper Industries has made innovations across virtually every facet of designing and manufacturing a front lamp assembly. Its headlamp for Dodge's Dakota and Durango models will be a new industry benchmark.

Wagner used proprietary software and rapid prototyping to provide customers with speedy feedback on feasibility and performance, shrinking the time from design to production. In addition, the resulting assembly has fewer parts, is lighter, has higher intrinsic quality, is easier to assemble and adjust, and achieves a more accurate fit and finish. It does not require horizontal aiming at the assembly stage, and due to other small but clever innovations, it simply does not leak, reducing a major source of warranty claims.

Wagner's lamp assembly doesn't feature whiz-bang technical breakthroughs. Rather, its collection of multiple innovations related in a superior product that brought significant commercial benefit to the company while exceeding customer performance expectations.

BENTELER AUTOMOTIVE

Thermally efficient, air-gap manifold and exhaust tube applications, parts, and systems.

Recognizing the need for improved thermal management to reduce emissions and underhood temperatures, Benteler pioneered the design and manufacture of air-gap, or dual-wall, exhaust manifolds. The innovation that earned Benteler a PACE Award is a dual-wall manifold design that provides a thin, decoupled liner with low thermal mass and rapid energy transfer to the catalytic converter. This enables reduced cold-start emissions due to improved "light off" times, thereby, avoiding more costly emission reduction technology, decreased catalyst size and previous metal content, and reduced overall system size and cost. The first application is in the Cadillac Northstar engine.

Development of this innovation required extraordinary cooperation between the customer and Benteler's experts in tool and die, stamping, engineering, hydroforming and manufacturing areas. This coordinated engineering effort provided immediate assurance that tight-tolerance designs were process-capable, on time, and within all cost and performance targets. Improved durability and NVH (noise, vibration, harshness) levels were achieved simultaneously.

Benteler is fully and strategically committed to air-gap systems, moving to nearly 100 percent production of these manifold products in the near future. This commitment reflects their customers' overwhelming acceptance of this technology and associated end products.

PRINCE, A JOHNSON CONTROLS COMPANY

CorteX® (trademark of Johnson Controls, Inc.), a unique, formable, energy-absorbing material for use in a car's overhead zone.

The Prince Division of Johnson Controls, Inc. has actually benefited from impending government regulation. It recognized early on that a new safety standard would legislate increased energy-absorption capabilities by interior trim, beginning with head impact to upper portions of a car's interior.

A Prince team proactively began developing an innovative solution to this legislation, which turned the problem into a success. The resulting innovation was CorteX, an energy-absorbing process and material that outperforms existing competitive impact-absorbing materials on relevant benchmarks at competitive costs, and exceeds federally mandated energy-absorption standards. In addition, CorteX is a composite blend of recycled roll fibers and thermoplastic material (PET), derived from used carpet and soft-drink bottles, and is itself completely recyclable. Once created, CorteX is readily formed over epoxy dies into unique, functional shapes to become dimensionally stable parts. These easily can be shaped to incorporate wire harnesses, structural clips, lights or other options, including hidden air passageways.

CorteX means both a lower-cost material and process that is applicable to other trim and energy-absorbing applications, such as door panels. The thickness of CorteX needed for the energy absorption required is less than that of conventional competitive materials, providing an interior space and visibility bonus, with no additional mass.

The culture, environment, and product development processes at Prince have made this kind of creativity the norm, in this case resulting in the possibility of a wide variety of high quality, low cost, recyclable, energy-absorbing products.

EATON CORPORATION, SPICER CLUTCH DIVISION

The industry's first adjustment-free clutch for heavy-duty truck applications.

Market surveys and customer inquiry showed that one of the most urgently needed developments in medium and heavy-duty truck fleet operation was low maintenance and adjustment-free clutches. The Eaton Corporation's Spicer Clutch Division capitalized on the opportunity, and has put into production the Eaton Spicer Solo, the first adjustment-free clutch for medium and heavy-duty truck fleets. With each push of the clutch pedal, a cam system and wear sensors check the clutch for wear and make any necessary adjustments.

The Eaton Spicer Solo system's wear-adjusting technology is based on two sliding cams. The clutch senses when wear calls for adjustment, and the cams rotate automatically to maintain proper adjustment throughout the life of the clutch. A wear indicator tab shows progressive cam movement, allowing easy monitoring of clutch wear without disassembly of the clutch.

This automatic adjustment innovation eliminates the need for manual clutch adjustment; increases useful life of the clutch, since it is always in correct adjustment; and substantially reduces maintenance downtime and labor. All of these factors reduce operating expense and improve truck fleet efficiency.

Because Eaton's Spicer Clutch Division is organized and motivated to identify opportunities and seek competitive advantage, it was able to create a product that is unique and commercially beneficial for itself and its customers. Market acceptance has been excellent in both OEM and after-market applications.

Notes

CHAPTER 1

1. Robert G. Cooper, "Stage-Gate Systems: A New Tool for Managing New Products," *Business Horizons,* May–June 1990, 44–54.
2. Scott Whitlock, from a speech at the PACE Automotive Innovation Forum, June 3, 1997.
3. As quoted in Joseph Pryweller, "Projects Could Turn Plastics into a Recycling Headliner," *Plastics News,* February 23, 1998.

CHAPTER 2

1. Gentex also produces fire protection products for commercial applications, including smoke detectors and audible and visual signaling devices, such as strobe warning lights, that are used in complete fire protection systems.
2. Peter F. Drucker, "The Discipline of Innovation," *Harvard Business Review,* November–December 1998, 156.
3. Robert Galvin, *The Idea of Ideas* (Chicago, IL: Motorola University Press, 1991), 36.

CHAPTER 3

1. See Edward E. Gordon, "Investing in Human Capital: The Case for Measuring Training ROI," *Corporate University Review,* January–February 1997.
2. For a more extensive description of Dana University, see Hallie Forcinio, "Dana University Ensures That Employees Find a Better Way," *Corporate University Review,* March–April 1997.
3. From Gentex Annual Report, 1998.
4. From John Teresko, "A Supplier on a Roll," *IndustryWeek,* March 2, 1998.

CHAPTER 4

1. Robert G. Cooper, "Stage-Gate Systems: A New Tool for Managing New Products," *Business Horizons,* May–June 1990, 44–54.
2. Glenn Omura, from a speech delivered at the PACE Automotive Innovation Forum, Dearborn, Michigan, June 3, 1997.
3. Jim Matheson and David Matheson, *The Smart Organization* (Boston, MA: Harvard Business School Publishing, 1998).
4. Marc H. Meyer and Alvin P. Lehnerd, *The Power of Product Platforms* (New York: The Free Press, 1997), xi–xii.
5. Office for the Study of Automotive Transportation, *Automotive Product Design and Development Delphi* (Ann Arbor: University of Michigan, Transport Research Institute, 1998), 11–15.
6. For a full discussion of the Swatch story, see William Taylor, "Message and Muscle: An Interview with Nicolas Hayek," *Harvard Business Review,* March–April 1993.

7. As told to the author by retired DaimlerChrysler executive, Glenn Gardner.
8. H. Kent Bowen, Kim B. Clark, Charles A. Holloway, and Steven C. Wheelwright, "Development Projects: The Engine of Renewal," *Harvard Business Review,* September–October 1994.

CHAPTER 5

1. Jim Matheson and David Matheson, *The Smart Organization* (Boston, MA: Harvard Business School Publishing, 1998), 5.

CHAPTER 6

1. Richard Foster, *Innovation: The Attacker's Advantage* (New York: Summit Books, 1986).
2. James M. Utterback, *Mastering the Dynamics of Innovation* (Boston, MA.: Harvard Business School Press, 1994), 158–59.
3. *PACE: What We've Learned So Far,* White Paper published by Ernst & Young, LLP.
4. Clayton M. Christensen, *The Innovator's Dilemma: When New Technologies Cause Great Firms to Fail* (Boston, MA.: Harvard Business School Press, 1997), ix.
5. From a web-published interview with Clayton Christensen, Harvard Business School Publishing, October 1998; www.harvard.edu/products/press/books/innovator/qa.html.
6. James R. Bright, "Evaluating Signals of Technological Change," *Harvard Business Review,* January–February 1970, 64.

7. See Robert Galvin, *The Idea of Ideas* (Chicago, IL: Motorola University Press, 1991), 95–95.
8. Utterback, *Mastering the Dynamics of Innovation,* 18.

CHAPTER 7

1. Joan Magretta, "Fast, Global, and Entrepreneurial: Supply Chain Management, Hong Kong Style: An Interview with Victor Fung," *Harvard Business Review,* September–October 1998, 105–6.
2. Gene Tyndall, Christopher Gopal, Wolfgang Partsch, and John Kamauff, *Supercharging Supply Chains* (New York: John Wiley & Sons, 1998), 8.
3. As described in Tyndall et al., ibid., 256.
4. Marshall L. Fisher, "What Is the Right Supply Chain for Your Product?" *Harvard Business Review,* March–April 1997, 106–16.
5. From PACE conference, Dearborn, Michigan, 1997.

CHAPTER 8

1. Rudy Ruggles, "Why Knowledge? Why Now?" *Prospectives on Business Innovation,* Issue 1, Ernst & Young Center for Business Innovation, 2.
2. Dorothy Leonard, *Wellsprings of Knowledge* (Boston, MA.: Harvard Business School Press, 1998), xi.
3. Ibid., 3.
4. Carla O'Dell and C. Jackson Greyson, Jr., *If Only We Knew What We Know* (New York: The Free Press, 1998), 8.
5. Joseph B. White, "The Line Starts Here, *Wall Street Journal,* January 11, 1999, R25.

6. As cited in O'Dell and C. Jackson Greyson, Jr., *If We Only Knew,* 153.
7. Thomas R. Davenport, "If Only HP Knew What HP Knows . . .," *Prospectives on Business Innovation,* Issue 1, Ernst & Young Center for Business Innovation, 20–25.
8. Richard Armstrong, "Managing Complex Knowledge at Bechtel," *Perspectives on Business Innovation,* Issue 1, Ernst & Young Center for Business Innovation, 53.

CHAPTER 9

1. See Joseph G. Morone, *Winning in High Tech Markets: The Role of General Management* (Boston, MA: Harvard Business School Press, 1993), 134–39.
2. Ibid., 135.
3. Steven C. Wheelwright and Kim B. Clark, *Leading Product Development* (New York: The Free Press, 1995), 22.
4. Robert Galvin, *The Idea of Ideas* (Chicago, IL: Motorola University Press, 1991), 95.
5. Jim Matheson and David Matheson, *The Smart Organization* (Boston, MA: Harvard Business School Press, 1998).
6. Clayton M. Christenson, *The Innovator's Dilemma* (Boston, MA: Harvard Business School Publishing, 1997), 99.

Index

Accelerated Solutions Environment™ (ASE), 97–100
Acer, 122
Adaptation, creative, 6–7
Aging of population (competition for best employees), 57–59
AirBus, 122
Alliances, 171
Alternatives, assessment of, 171
Altshuller, Genrikh, 49
Amazon, 139, 140
American Production Quality Center (APQC), 144, 147, 149
Analytical tools, 67
Armistead, William, 161
Armstrong, Richard, 157
Arriortua, Jose Ignacio Lope de, 124
ASHA Corporation, 104, 210–211
Assembly line (near-future scenario), 197–202
AT&T, 106, 122
Auto-Clear™ Rain Sensor, 119, 120
Automotive industry:
  defining characteristics (three), 177–178
  example, supply chain innovation, 127–132
  innovation in (*see* Innovation)
  Internet/e-commerce, 3, 4, 112, 131, 139–140, 157, 204–205
  manufacturing models, traditional, 199
  Pace Awards (*see* Pace Awards)
Automotive industry: future scenario: Connected Car Company (Appendix A), 177–208
  assembly line, 197–202
  car buyers, 179–185
  computers and communications, 205–206
  connected value web (suppliers), 195–197
  connectivity, 178, 206
  delivery, 202–204
  engineering team, 194–195
  intangible value, 178
  marketing executive, 185–190
  push/pull system of planning and order filling, 206
  speculations, 206–208
  speed, 177–178, 206
  value of intangibles, 206

Automotive Network Exchange (ANX) system, 131
Awards:
 Golden Lemon, 173
 Golden Step, 34
 Pace (*see* Pace Awards)
 Purple Thumb, 173

Badawy, Aly, 162
Ballard, 116
Ballmer, Steve, 17
Barabba, Vincent, 110
Barrier blasting, 31
Bauer, Fred, 23, 27, 31, 33, 34, 35, 36, 37, 39, 42, 45, 78, 91, 164, 169, 172
Benchmarking, 35, 57, 148–149, 156
 exercises, 57
 Motorola, 35
 powerful tool of knowledge management, 148–149
 Xerox, 156
Benteler Automotive Corporation, 48, 211–212, 222–223
Big markets, focus on, 110–111
"Black box" designs, 22, 72
Black & Decker, 70, 125, 162
BMW, 28, 153
Boeing, 99, 122, 124
Bottom-up innovation, 163–165
Bowen, Kent, 60
Bright, James R., 111
Business evaluation (in innovation process), 13
Business improvement (requirement for innovation), 9–10

Cadillac Northstar, 222
CALL (U.S. Army's Center for Army lessons Learned), 154
Car buyers, future scenario, 179–185
Carlson Companies, 99
Carlton, Richard P., 34
Catalytic converters, 3, 9–10, 142
Champions/believers, partnership of, 169–170
Chevron, 147, 156
Christensen, Clay, 108, 111, 173
Chrysler, 28, 29, 50, 80–83, 94, 109, 122, 128, 129, 212. *See also* DaimlerChrysler
 Dodge Dakota, 138, 221
 Dodge Durango, 221
Clark, Kim, 60, 166
Closed loop systems, 15
Clutch Division, Eaton, 224–225
Codifying knowledge, 150, 159
COIN. *See* Communities of interest (COINs)
Colocation, 78
Comfort Engineering Laboratory (JCI), 101–103. *See also* Johnson Controls, Inc. (JCI)
Command/control *vs.* learning/innovation, 55
Communities of interest (COINs), 155–157, 159
Company assessment:
 innovation-friendly environment, 45–46
 innovative capabilities, 25–26
 knowledge management, 158–159
 new product development, 84
 supply chain, 139
Company size, and innovation, 53–54, 174
Compaq, 8, 106, 122
Competition:
 changing basis of (requirement for innovation), 7–9
 nature of changing, 122
Computer(s):
 design/modeling/CAD, 73, 103
 future of, 205–206
 and Internet (*see* Internet/ e-commerce)
 on-board (auto), 3
 simulations, 73
Connectivity:
 defining characteristic (one of three) of automotive industry, 178

in lockstep with speed (speculations on future), 206
trend driving innovation, 5
Control Devices, Inc., 119, 120
Cooper, Robert G., 13, 62, 63, 66
Cooper Automotive, Wagner Lighting Division, 221–222
Corning Incorporated, 9–10, 24, 60, 161, 174
CorteX®, 15, 223–224
Creativity *vs.* innovation, 6
Culture as obstacle to innovation and knowledge management, 157
Customer(s):
adoption by (requirement for innovation), 7
customer-pull operation, 90
listening too closely to, 109
listening to right (innovators, lead users, opinion leaders), 110

Daewoo, 28, 205
DaimlerChrysler, 15, 44, 74, 79, 81, 82, 117, 138, 150–153, 172, 205, 210. *See also* Chrysler
Engineering Books of Knowledge (EBOKs), 150–151, 152
Supplier Book of Knowledge (SBOK), 151, 152
"Tech Clubs," 82, 151
Web site GetaQuote, 205
Dana Corporation, 36, 40, 50–54, 89–91, 101, 112, 114–118, 126, 138, 147, 165
Darden School study, 132–134
Davenport, Tom, 150
Decision making, processes for, 97, 171
Delivery (near-future scenario), 202–204
Dell Computer Corporation, 8, 106, 122, 126, 137, 139, 140, 196, 197
Delphi Automotive Systems (Delphi Saginaw Steering Systems), 1, 2, 40, 44, 108, 119, 147, 161–162, 212–213
Demand-pull manufacturing operation, 38
Deming, W. Edwards, 19, 39, 100
Dialogue decision process, 171
Digital Equipment Corporation, 110
Digital imaging, 113
Discontinuous/incremental innovation, 10–12
Dodge Dakota, 138, 221
Dodge Durango, 221
Drucker, Peter, 37, 174
DTE Energy Company, 116
Dual career ladders, 34–36
Dürr Industries, Inc., 42–44, 220–221

Eastman, George, 25
Eastman Kodak, 24–25, 80, 113, 134
Eaton Corp., Spicer Clutch Division, 224–225
e-commerce (trend driving innovation), 4. *See also* Internet/e-commerce
ECT (emerging core technologies), 115–117
Edison, Thomas, 6, 24, 41
Efficiency in new product development, 73–79
Electric vehicles (EVs), 116–118
Electrochromics, 28–29, 42, 91, 219–220
Employee(s). *See* People/employee(s)
EMT (extended mobility technology), 104. *See also* Goodyear Tire & Rubber Company
Engineering team (near-future scenario), 194–195
Enterprise resource planning (ERP), 77, 151
Ernst & Young:
Accelerated Solutions Environment™ (ASE), 97–100
communities of interest (COINs), 156

Ernst & Young *(Continued)*
Concept Automobile Industry Project, 177
knowledge management, 142, 144, 148, 151–152, 153, 156, 158
new product design study, 73
performance metrics: process/results, 158
spatial relationships experiment, 153
supply chain study, 132–134
E-Steer™. *See* Delphi Automotive Systems (Delphi Saginaw Steering Systems)
Evans, Rob, 99

Failure:
bringing closer to success (Edison), 41
cultivating art of cheap, 170
eliminating fear of, 39–44
making most of inevitable, 173
Federal Express, 199–200, 202
Fiat, 2, 28, 213
Fiber optics, 60, 161
Fisher, Marshall, 135
Fiz Center (BMW), 153
Ford, 15, 18–19, 28, 44, 74, 113, 117, 118, 122, 148–149, 197, 199, 205, 212
Ford, Henry, 197
Ford models:
Escort, 212
Taurus, 19
Windstar, 211
Forward looking, 172–173
Foster, Richard, 1, 106
Fuel cell technology, 113, 116–117
Fung, Victor, 122, 123, 124
Future scenario, automotive industry: Connected Car Company, 177–208

Galvin, Robert, 41, 167
Gardner, Glenn, 80, 81, 82–83
Gates, Bill, 17, 188
Gateway, 139, 140
General Electric, 9, 50, 53, 117, 174
General Motors (GM), 2, 28, 44, 68, 74, 94, 95, 117, 122, 124, 128, 171, 205, 213
Internet-based car-selling service (GM BuyPower), 205
Motors Delta platform (Sunfire/Cavalier), 2, 213
Gentex Corporation, 23, 27–45, 52–53, 78, 91–92, 164, 171, 219–220
GERODISC™, 104, 210–211
GetaQuote (DaimlerChrysler), 205
Giantism, corporate (antidote), 53–54
Globalization (trend driving innovation), 4
GM. *See* General Motors (GM)
Golden Step Award, 34
Goodyear Tire & Rubber Company, 72, 104, 213–214
Gopal, Chris, 99
Grace Construction Product Division, 65–67, 68, 69
"Gray box" development, 72
Greyson, C. Jackson, Jr., 147, 149
Grove, Andy, 44

Handy, Charles, 47
Headlamps, 221–222
Hewlett, Bill, 17
Hewlett-Packard (HP), 17, 60, 70, 77, 122, 124–125, 137, 150, 155, 173, 174
Hippel, Eric von, 110
Holloway, Charles, 60
HomeLink® Universal transceiver, 13–14
Honda, 28, 74, 142
Hughes Aircraft, 162
Hydro-mechanical coupling device (GERODISC™), 104, 210–211

IBM, 8, 34, 68, 79–80, 106, 110, 133, 137
ILP. *See* Invention Leadership Program (ILP)
Improvement *vs.* innovation, 12
Incremental/discontinuous innovation, 10–12

Industry relationships, greater share of (reward of innovation), 22
Information flow, 54–57
old and new (Figure 3.2), 56
Information systems *vs.* effective knowledge management, 159
Innovation, 1–26
cost of, 10, 169
discontinuous *vs.* incremental, 10–12
encouraging (*see* Innovation-friendly environment)
individuals (spark of depending on), 47–48
key to sustaining/winning, 174–175
knowledge, managing/applying, 141–159
leadership in, 160–173
in organizational processes, 96–100
people (*see* People/employee(s))
as process, 12–18
process (*see* Process innovation)
product, 60–84 (*see also* New product development (NPD))
supply chain, 122–140 (*see also* Supplier(s))
technology (*see* Technology and innovation)
true, *vs.* refinement/improvement, 3
Innovation: definition (Pace Awards program: four requirements), 5–10
Innovation: definition (Schumpeter's), 106
Innovation, rewards of, 18–22
quality, 20
sales from new products, 20
sales growth, 19–20
speed, 20–21
Innovation, trends driving need for, 3–4
connectivity, 5
e-commerce, 4
globalization, 4
power of new products, 4–5
supply chain cost reduction, 5
Innovation building block (three-dimensional model), 22–25, 174
people (*see* People/employee(s))
process (*see* Process innovation)
technology (*see* Technology and innovation)
Innovation dilemma, 108–109, 111
Innovation-friendly environment, 27–46, 168, 175
approaches, five (listed), 30
attracting innovative people, 36–39
barrier blasting, 31
dual career ladders, 34–36
fear, eliminating, 39–44
organizational discomfort, 44–45
outward-looking company, 35
recognition, 30
rewards/recognition, 31–36
suggestion systems, 36
top-level commitment, forms of, 30–31
visibility of leadership, 30, 81–82
Innovators, listening to customers who are, 110
Intangibles, value of, 178, 206
Intel®, 44, 106, 201
Internet/e-commerce, 3, 4, 112, 131, 139–140, 157, 204–205
Invention Leadership Program (ILP), 49
Inventory, 130, 136
i2 Technologies (Dallas Texas), 76

Jachimowicz, Felek, 65–66, 67
Jet propulsion (example of discontinuous innovation), 10
Johnson, Cindy, 149
Johnson Controls, Inc. (JCI), 8–9, 13, 52, 68, 101–103, 171
Comfort Engineering Laboratory, 101–103
Quest, 52
Jones, Chuck, 40, 101, 114, 116, 117, 118
Jones, Peter, 93–94

Just-in-time Toyota production system, 91

Kaizen, 12
Kanban system, 87
Karney, Bruce, 150
Klann, Bill, 148, 149
KM. *See* Knowledge management (KM)
Knowledge management (KM), 141–159, 168, 175
  assessing your company, 158–159
  CALL (Center for Army Lessons Learned), 154
  communities of interest (COINs), 155–157
  data (defined), 144
  definition of terms, 144
  elimination of waste, 155
  explicit knowledge, 143
  information (defined), 144
  and innovation, 154–158
  intellectual capital (defined), 144
  knowledge (defined), 144
  obstacles, 157–158
  performance metrics, 158
  reshaping corporation with, 145
  spatial relationships matter, 153
  tacit knowledge, 143, 144, 152–154, 155–156, 159
Knowledge management (KM): process, 145–154
  applying/reusing, 151–154
  benchmarking, 148–149
  capturing/generating, 146–148
  diagram (Figure 8.1), 146
  storing, 149–151
Kodak, 80, 113, 134. *See also* Eastman Kodak
Koop, Brian, 160

Large companies, 53–54, 174
Leadership, 160–173
  bottom-up innovation, 163–165
  senior management involvement in development projects (Figure 9.2), 167
  strategic direction, 163–165
  top-down innovation, 160–163
Leadership: executive role, 166–173
  creating alternative paths forward, 168
  creating partnership of champions/believers, 169–170
  cultivating art of cheap failures, 170
  getting people to look outward, 171–172
  looking beyond current ideas to superior alternatives, 171
  looking forward not backward, 172–173
  looking for opportunities to say yes, 169
  making most of inevitable failures, 173
  using alliances when necessary, 171
  willingness to pay for innovation, 169
Lead users, 110
Learning environment, 83–84
Leonard, Dorothy, 141, 143, 145
LH Platform Team, 55, 80–83. *See also* Chrysler
Li & Fung, 123, 124, 139
Light bulbs, 9
Lincoln Navigator, 218
Longaberger, Dave (Longaberger Basket), 38
Look-back bonuses, 30, 33
Lotus Notes, 150, 157
Lutz, Robert, 81–82, 109, 172
Lynch, Peter, 28

Mack truck, 126
Management:
  change, 120–121
  involvement in development projects (Figure 9.2), 167
  knowledge (*see* Knowledge management (KM))
  portfolio (and limited resources), 69

role of (*see* Leadership)
supply (*see* Supply management)
Management by wandering around, 173
Managing people *vs.* managing processes, 100
Manifold design, 222
Marketing executive (near-future scenario), 185–190
Mass customization, 90
Matheson, David, 69, 96–97, 171
Matheson, James, 69, 96–97, 171
MCI, 122
Mechanical Technology, Inc., 116
Mercedes-Benz, 15, 28, 219
Meritor Automotive, Inc., 214–215
Meynell, David, 43, 44
Microsoft, 17, 60, 106
Military, 78–79, 154
Miniaturization, 3, 11
Modularity, 71
Monroe Auto Equipment, 35, 62, 88–89
Morcott, Woody, 54, 138
Morone, Joseph, 161
Motorola, 30, 35, 38, 41, 49, 50, 56, 57, 71–72, 105–106, 113–114, 133–134, 165, 167, 171, 174, 216–217
Invention Leadership Program (ILP), 49
MPC555 PowerPC microcontroller with embedded flash memory, 105–106, 216
Technology Roadmap Program, 113–114, 165

NASA:
Apollo program (metaphor for role of knowledge in commercial competition), 142–143
Naval engineers, 78–79
Negative working capital, 140
New product(s), power of: trend driving innovation, 4–5
New product development (NPD), 60–84, 175
cost of long cycles, 75
leadership in (reward of innovation), 21–22
as learning lab, 83–84
platform power, 70–72
process example (Grace Construction), 65–68
relationship between product/process innovation, 87
stage-gate process (*see* Stage-gate process)
supplier role, 72, 73
teams, 79–83
using process for, 62–65
what process can't do, 68–69
New product development (NPD): speed/efficiency, 73–79
colocation, 78
data integration, 76–77
expectations, 78–79
optimizing development activities, 74–76
postponement, 77–78
Night Vision Safety® (NVS) mirrors. *See* Gentex Corporation
Nissan, 28, 74
NUMMI (New United Motor Manufacturing Inc.), 90, 91

O'Dell, Carla, 147, 149
Office layout, and knowledge management, 153
Omura, Glenn, 64, 68, 69
Opel, 2, 28, 162, 213
Opinion leaders (customers), 110
Optimization of product schedules, 76
Organizational discomfort, 44–45
Organizational processes, innovations in, 96–100. *See also* Process innovation
Outward looking people/company, 35, 171–172
Oven designs. *See* Dürr Industries, Inc.

Pace Awards:
  judged on three dimensions (leadership, uniqueness, results), 209
  recipients, 1998-1999 (Appendix B), 209–225
  rigorous definition of innovation, 5–10
Pace Awards: four requirements for innovation, 5–10
  adopted by customers, 7
  changes basis of competition, 7–9
  has not been seen before, 5–7
  transforms innovator's business for better, 9–10
Packard-Bell, 122
Paint-baking ovens. *See* Dürr Industries, Inc.
PalmPilot, 72
PDP. *See* Product development process (PDP)
People/employee(s), 23, 36–39, 47–59, 100, 168, 172, 175
  attracting innovative people, 36–39
  competition for best, 57–59
  dimension of innovation, 23
  maximizing potential, 47–59, 168, 175
  opening flow of information, 54–57
  "repotting," 57, 172
  rewards/recognition, 31–36
  spirit of participation, 52–54
  suggestion systems, 12, 36
  training/education, 48–52, 57, 172
People-to-documents approach, 152
Personal computers (PCs), cost/performance improvements since 1995, 3
Peugeot-Citroën, 96
Pfizer, 60
Photographic innovations, 25. *See also* Eastman Kodak
Plate glass process, 85–86
Platforms, 70–72
Plug Power, 116, 117
Pointer system, 155
Polaroid, 80
Poole, Ralph, 156
Postponement, 77–78
Powdered metal (PM) parts, 92–96, 217–218
Power Plug, 117
Prince Corporation, 13, 223–224. *See also* Johnson Controls, Inc. (JCI)
Problem solving, processes for, 97
Process innovation, 85–100
  and competitive excellence, 88–91
  innovation building block, 24
  managing people *vs.* managing processes, 100
  organizational processes, 96–100
  product-process connection, 87, 91–96
  seeking opportunities for, 175
Product(s), functional *vs.* innovative, and supply chain, 135–136
Product development process (PDP), 65–66. *See also* New product development (NPD)
Product innovation. *See* New product development (NPD)
Production ramp up and marketing (in innovation process), 13
Product platform, 70–72
Profitability (reward of innovation), 22
Profit-sharing system, 32
Prototyping, virtual, 73
Prototyping (in innovation process), 13
Push planning system, 196
Push/pull system of planning and order filling, 206

Qualitative evaluation stage, 65
Quality (reward of innovation), 19, 20

Quality circles, 12
Quality performance measures (Figure 1.3), 20
Quantitative tools, 67

Radiant Floor Construction (RFC) paint oven. *See* Dürr Industries, Inc.
Recognition and qualitative evaluation (in innovation process), 13, 16–18
Recognition/rewards, 30, 31–36
Recognizor role, 16–17, 64, 163
Recyclable materials, 15, 119, 224
Remote entry function, home lighting/security, 7, 13–14
Resources, limited (prioritization/portfolio management), 69
RHP Highway Parallelogram Trailer Air Suspension System, 214–215
Risk, 37, 173
Ruggles, Rudy, 142
Run Flat Eagle Fl GS EMT tire technology. *See* Goodyear Tire & Rubber Company
Runkle, Don, 1, 161

Saab of Santa Ana, California, 204–205
Saginaw Steering. *See* Delphi Automotive Systems (Delphi Saginaw Steering Systems)
Sales from new products (reward of innovation), 20
Sales growth (reward of innovation), 19–20
Scanning, 111–113, 121, 165
Scientific Advisor Board Associates (SABA), 57
Seat Innovation Team (SIT), 16
Selective densification (SelectDens™), 92, 95, 217–218
Sharfman, William, 138
SIT team. *See* Seat Innovation Team (SIT)
SmithKline Beecham, 171
Societé Micromécanique et Horlogäre (SMH), 77
Space program. *See* NASA
Spatial relationships, and knowledge management, 153
Speed/efficiency, 20–21, 73–79, 177–178, 206
  colocation, 78
  data integration, 76–77
  expectations, 78–79
  optimizing development activities, 74–76
  postponement, 77–78
  supply chain (and product type), 135–136
Stackpole, Limited, 92–96, 217–218
Stage-gate process, 13, 62–66, 75–76
  generic (Figure 4.2), 62
  participants, 64
Standardization, 200
Stock option programs, 33
Strategy:
  innovation *vs.* improvements, 12
  innovation linkage (Figure 9.1), 165
  strategic direction, 163–165
Suggestion systems, 12, 36
Suman, Mike, 9, 16, 103, 169
Supplier(s):
  role in new product development, 72, 73
  and Toyota Production System (TPS): no margin for error, 91
Supply chain, innovation in, 5, 122–140, 175
  auto industry example, 127–132
  broader view of competition, 122
Supply chain cost reduction (trend driving innovation), 5
Supply management:
  cost of, 136
  defined, 124–125
  improvements in, value of, 132–134
  old *vs.* new models (lists), 125
Supply-push concept, 90

Supply web, 5, 123, 125, 126, 131
  collaboration, 125–132
  evolutionary path (Figure 7.1), 126
  near-future scenario, 195–197
  right one for your business, 134–137
  your challenge: get connected, 139–140
Support, official/unofficial, 163
Swatch Watch, 70, 77

Tacit knowledge, 143, 144, 152–154, 155–156, 159
Teams, 79–83
  communication, 82
  LH Platform Team, 80–83
  success factors, 81–83
  Team Zebra, 80
Technofusion, 118–120, 175
Technology, locking in old, 75
Technology and innovation, 14, 24–25, 75, 101–121, 162, 205–206, 207
  bridging discontinuities, 106–111
  change management, 120–121
  dimension of innovation, 24–25
  future speculations, 205–206
  integration of multiple capabilities, 119
  leadership, 162
  payoff, 105
  perils/promise, 120–121
  process, 113–118
  scanning, 111–113, 121
  unfavorable business practices, 109–110
Teleflex, Inc. (Teleflex Automotive Group), 218–219
Tenneco, 62, 88
Testing/validation (in innovation process), 13
Texas Instruments, 147–148, 149
Theory-of-Constraints (TOC), 76
Theory of Inventive Problem Solving, 49
3M, 6, 24, 34–36, 41, 53, 60, 68, 124, 156, 168, 174
Time/money, obstacle to effective knowledge management, 157
Time Warner, 190
Top-down innovation, 160–163
Top-level commitment, forms of, 30–31
Tosch, Paul, 1, 162
Toyota, 8, 28, 50, 74, 86–87, 89, 90, 117, 199
Toyota Production System (TPS), 8, 86–87, 90, 91
Toyota Tacoma, 90
Training/education, 48–52, 57, 172
Transistor (example of discontinuous innovation), 11
TRW, 119
Tupperware, 38
Typewriter, 119–120
"Tyranny of the served market," 110

Utterback, James, 85, 87, 106, 108, 119

Valuation of technology, analytical tools for, 67
Value Web,™ 123, 124, 127, 128, 131, 132, 134–139
Vehicle teardown, 74
Virtual prototyping, 73
Volkswagen, 2, 213

Wagner Lighting Division, Cooper Automotive, 221–222
Wal-Mart, 100, 137, 202
Wheelwright, Steven, 60, 166
Whitlock, Scott, 14
Wilkie, Brian, 41, 56, 72
WIN88 rear twist beam axle for 1998 Ford Windstar, 211–212

Xerox, 156

Yorktown, 78–79
Younger workers, attracting/optimizing, 59

Zip drive, example of true innovation, 3